Softer Success

PREVENT BURNOUT, FIND BALANCE

AND RE-DEFINE YOUR SUCCESS

by Cara de Lange

BE MORE GENTLE WITH YOURSELF

Dedication

My darling Arianna & Natalia; you are my inspiration

This book is for you if you...

- want to re-establish success for yourself;

- would like to create more balance in your life but don't know how;

- want to learn how to be more gentle with yourself;

- are feeling overwhelmed or stressed or close to burnout;

- you are doing everything for everybody and always putting yourself last on the list and

- you are a professional, entrepreneur, mother or working mother who wants to achieve a greater success in your life by being more gentle with yourself

A Note to YOU the Reader

Before you start reading this book, I wanted to let you know that it is written with love and shares my personal story. It shares with you the most amazing thing I have discovered in my life; how to live a Softer Success. Please read on and discover a Softer Success for your life too.

I invite you to practise a short visualisation with me ... or if you struggle with visualising, grab a pen and paper and start writing.

Firstly, sit in a comfortable position and close your eyes. Take a deep breath. Look at your life. Just for a moment. See your life in front of you like a movie. Or, a static picture of a movie. See everything that is going on in your life at the moment. Is it moving too fast? Do you feel you could slow down? How do you feel about your life? Are you happy? Are you unhappy? Are you content? Or frustrated? Are you too hard on yourself? Take time to think about how you feel about your life, right now.

Secondly, take another deep breath. Keep your eyes closed. See a different life in front of you like movie. Imagine what your life could look like if there was a greater softness to it? If you are being softer every day in everything you do. How might your life look and feel? Are you able to be more gentle with yourself? What does softness mean for you? Write down what you see and feel about a softer, more gentle life and what it could mean to you.

I am guessing that you are reading this book because you want to change something in your life. You might want to learn how to approach stress in a different way, to have less overwhelm or stress in your life and to learn to slow down. Maybe, you are already practising self-care and want to learn more. Perhaps, you have managed to slow down, but want to know additional, different techniques. Or maybe, you are interested in my story about how to prevent burnout.

Why would you adopt a Softer Success approach? What could this do for you? And what would this mean for you? How could your life look and feel if it was softer? Might there be less guilt in your life? Could you be looking after yourself better? Are you saying 'no' to things? Could you feel more peaceful and relaxed?

I wrote *Softer Success* to help you.

Now, I hear you. You may be thinking that there is already so much to do every day. I don't need to know more tips nor be given more changes to make, which might overwhelm you.

However, this book is not about adding more things to do in your existing, busy life. You are already doing great! I wrote this book because I'm passionate about preventing women from experiencing stress and burnout by teaching them to be more gentle with themselves. To use your energy in a more productive way. This book will help you to take a look at your life in a different way and learn about a softer way that you can live your life.

I share my personal story to show you that you can be more powerful, but in a softer way and you can be more successful, but by taking care of you own needs first. I invite you to take a look at your life to see what you need to change to live a more peaceful and nourished life. This book gives you all you need to be more gentle with yourself and to lead to a life of Softer Success, as I have done.

We live in a busy world and it is only getting busier. Something needs to change before burnout and depression becomes epidemic.

I weave my personal story throughout this book and it is my intention that some of these stories will make you chuckle. The three question exercises and practical tips you will find in every chapter are easy to dip in and out of. Even if you only adopt one or two of them, they will start leading you towards a more peaceful life and a Softer Success.

Please enjoy this book and let me know how you get on. My contact details are at the back of the book and I would love to hear about your personal Softer Success.

With love for a Softer Success.
Cara de Lange

What People Are Saying About This Book

'A subtle, sensible and sensitive book that gently reframes how we might look at the world of work in order to enjoy success that's not just softer, but perhaps even more sustainable, too.'

Professor Andrew Sharman,
author of _The Wellbeing Book_ and _Working Well_

'If you want to avoid burnout, being kind to yourself is the way to go. **Softer Success** captures this principle beautifully and ticks off all the important aspects. Cara's Three Question Exercises will get you thinking, and the Practical Tips will guide you on your journey. Not only does **Softer Success** explain how to protect yourself but it also shows you how to be a role model for the next generation, an added bonus in this crazy world.'

Susan Scott, Mind Body Expert, Business Psychologist

'A wonderful kind, wise yet light-hearted book! It really does help you become more successful and powerful by learning to be more gentle with yourself. If we all adopted a **'Softer Success'** there would be much less stress around. I love Cara's personal anecdotes 'Nerdy Girl'. The book also highlights how much hormones can have an effect on women's lives and Cara demonstrates her first-hand experience. I will recommend this book to all women who are feeling stressed, overwhelmed and want to prevent burnout. A helpful and brilliant book.'

Nicki Williams, Nutritionist and Hormone Expert

'In this fast paced world in which we live, Cara's book on being kinder to yourself if a timely reminder on how to minimise stress and prevent burnout. A good easy read and a welcome addition to the bookshelf.'

Carole Spiers, CEO Carole Spiers Group

'A relevant and timely book for today's busy world. More than ever before we need to pause and redefine what success actually means for ourselves. Cara's book is a great example how we can turn our challenges into life-changing and life-affirming events. She took her own experience of burnout and turned it into a resource for other women to start loving themselves more deeply. It provides the younger generation with true life examples of how to live wisely. Thank you, Cara for this amazing book! Many women will find relief and inspiration in your valuable advice.'

Gosia Gorna, Transformational Coach, Author and Speaker

'In her excellent book **Softer Success**, Cara de Lange has created a wonderful template for women to live successfully. Her focus on PMT, pregnancy and menopause will help many women understand their bodies better and the hormonal effects. Her self-help advice is impressive, as is the recognition that transdermal hormones can remove depression in women without resorting to antidepressants. For example, this protection of the women's mood during a lengthy period of breast feeding is certainly true, but it is not always recognised.'

John STUDD, DSc, MD, FRCOG, Professor of Gynaecology

'An amazing and inspiring book! So powerful and a great reminder to be kinder to ourselves. Written in a very natural way, easy to read and relate to. Very funny too which I love! I love the Nerdy Girl stories, they really made me chuckle.'

Elisabeth Brind, Director, World First

Foreword

By Dr Nerina Ramlakhan, Physiologist, Sleep and Stress Management Expert and published author

I first met Cara years ago when she came to see me for help with her insomnia. I remember her distinctly. She was immaculately made up and beautifully dressed. She sat perfectly straight and upright, hardly moving as she spoke. There was a rigidity in her posture and demeanour and I wasn't surprised she couldn't sleep. After all, sleep is an act of letting go and softening. It has been a privilege to watch her soften and share her journey in this book. It is greatly needed.

Being a woman in today's world is hard. That is not to say that being a man in today's world isn't hard but for women, we are living in unprecedented times. Our mothers and foremothers had it hard too, but it was a different type of hard. My mother worked in a factory stacking heavy boxes when she was heavily pregnant carrying me in her belly. Her mother and my grandmother worked in the rice and sugar plantations in Guyana, wielding cutlasses and harvesting the crops under the fierce tropical sun. Without a doubt, these women had to be tough. My life couldn't be more different. I am a mother and successful businesswoman. I make my own money, travel extensively and pay my own bills. I have a great deal of freedom to choose my relationships and to reach for personal fulfilment.

Never have we women in the West had more opportunity, more choice, more freedom. Yes, we still have a way to go, but in comparison to any other time in history, we have never had so much freedom to create our own destinies and forge our way ahead.

But it continues to be hard. With all of these roles and options comes a sense of overwhelm and confusion. I have witnessed this in the twenty five years of doing my work and my sleep practice is busy! It is great that we have choices, but it is not so great that with them comes a deluge of must do's, should do's, have to do's. In this age of excessive leaning in, every 'yes' becomes a 'no' to something else. Never before, have we needed so much to stop, slow down and discern. And when we don't, we become hard, rigid, tight in the neck and shoulders, clenched in the jaw, tense in the belly and sleepless. This hardness blocks our life force. It stops us reaching our potential. It stops us feeling and living a radiant life.

Cara de Lange learned first-hand the effects of this hardening and in her book she shares her personal story with compassion, humour and courage. Most importantly, she shares her journey of learning how to lean back, soften and allow gentleness. Her aim is to liberate women from the excessive effort and pushing that can so easily become habitual and exhausting not only for us, but also for those people we love and care about. In this technologically driven, demanding world we live in, a great deal of softness is needed, and not only for women. Men yearn for it too and our children especially need it. There is a magic that happens when we drop the unnecessary effort and allow ourselves to soften. I have witnessed this not only with my patients and clients, but by experiencing it myself.

Cara maps out a way of finding this softness and she shares tools that are simple and practical but, at the same time, profound.

If your life is already swamped by demand and 'have to do's' the last thing you need is yet another book to clutter your bedside table. However, every lesson, every story and every technique shared in this book can bring softer success that doesn't come at a personal cost. Be prepared to feel the return of your true power, energy and *joie de vivre*.

Nerina Ramlakhan PhD

Contents

CHAPTER 1. You Have Changed...25

CHAPTER 2. Talk to Other People...39

CHAPTER 3. Stop Fighting...49

CHAPTER 4. Take Time for Yourself...59

CHAPTER 5. Pretty Lady...69

CHAPTER 6. Fire The Good Girl...79

CHAPTER 7. Structure for Wellbeing...89

CHAPTER 8. Be Kind 99

CHAPTER 9. Connect With Other Women...109

Epilogue; Softer Success Redefined **119**

Contact Cara **121**

Chapter References **123**

Recommended Additional Reading **127**

Softer Success Workshop Feedback **129**

Acknowledgements **131**

About The Author **133**

Introduction:
A Kinder, Gentler Philosophy on Success

Success, what does it really mean?

We often define success by what we are told via social media, marketing, the news and our peers. Often, it means earning more money or being famous. These days, society in general expects us to have everything; family, a career and a beautiful body and we push ourselves to the limits to get there. But what if we were to look inwardly to find the meaning of success? If we defined success for ourselves, what would that be? Maybe, success actually means looking after ourselves first. Success; meaning creating a balance for ourselves and having a healthy mind and body; being more gentle and caring towards ourselves, as well as other people.

Modern day philosopher, Alain de Botton promotes the concept of, "a kinder, gentler philosophy of success" and in particular talked about this topic in his Ted Talk, July 2009. He believes that modern society tends to worship themselves in contrast to all other societies who have had something else to worship, such as a God, spirit, the divine force or the universe etc. He suggests that while we may have lost the habit of worshipping a divine force, modern society is drawn towards nature. We enjoy looking at oceans and glaciers, where we can relate to something else. Nature is an escape from our daily competition and life's dramas.

When we talk about success and failure, we think we know what success means. When we are told someone is successful we immediately think it's because they have made a lot of money or are renowned in their field. However, Alain de Botton's theory about success is that you can't be successful at everything. We hear about work life balance and how you can have it all. But can we really? Alain de Botton believes that any vision of success has to admit that there is also an element of loss. Any wise person will accept there are going to be areas where they are not succeeding. Actually, we should never give up on our individual ideas of success. By focusing on them, we can make sure they are truly our own ambitions and not what society tells us or expects of us. Success yes, but let's accept the individual nature of success and make sure that our ideas are truly our own. This means we can take a softer approach to success by redefining it with our own unique meaning.

I believe this is a very healthy approach. Our ideas of success are often not our own. They are sucked in from other people's beliefs. Often, they stem from our parents. We are also influenced by the press, radio, television, advertising and social media. These are hugely invasive messages that can start to define what we want and how we view ourselves. For example, when we are told that a person is a 'celebrity' we automatically see them as successful. We are highly open to suggestions.

For me, success used to be about pushing myself. Working too hard, working even harder, being tough on myself and tough on other people. I wanted to be superwoman. I compared myself to other people and thought I needed to work harder to achieve success.

But what if there is actually a softer kind of success, where you put yourself and your needs first; where you can be more gentle with yourself?

The question is – how do you do that? It can seem unattainable with all the stresses in life. But it is possible and I will show you how to achieve that in this book.

By being more gentle with yourself and changing your mindset you can achieve a type of success that is much more sustainable. Too many people these days are burning out. It is a clear indication that we have to change the way we live and slow down. By slowing down and looking after yourself, miracles can happen and you will find a Softer Success.

I invite you to come on a journey with me to a Softer Success.

My Story

"My burnout was devastating but it was a wake call and paradoxically lead me to discover my life's work and passion"

So how did it all start?

When I was pregnant with my first daughter, I was determined to continue working at the same fast pace, or even a bit faster. I had been challenging myself too much and had a real wake-up call one day when I met my husband and some friends at a restaurant after a long day at work. I was working full-time at a top global technology company as an Executive Assistant and it was a very busy job. It was wintertime and when I arrived at the restaurant and walked in from the cold, I fainted. The restaurant called an ambulance because I was 22 weeks pregnant and I was taken off to hospital. There was a midwife in the ambulance who told me I was really lucky because I could have had my baby on the spot! The midwife told me to slow down and when I told her I had a busy full-time job at a global technology company and that was impossible ... she gave me a stern look and I knew I had to take her advice seriously. I had to change something. Once back at work, I started to handover a few tasks to my colleague and to slow down generally and look after myself better.

This was a wake-up call. I took it seriously to start with, but once my second child came along it was much harder to stick to 'slowing down'.

Then one day in 2015 it hit me. Burnout. With a capital B. Attending meetings had me in a sweat. I felt tired but wired at the same time. I struggled; really struggled with daily tasks. Giving my kids a bath left me feeling exhausted. I suffered insomnia. I started to feel anxious. It was a slow burner that I had been absolutely oblivious to. My shoulders were tight and I had back and neck pain. I was rigid with stress which I'd been holding inside my body instead of expressing my emotions.

I needed a new strategy. I was not going to recover if I did not radically change my way of thinking and doing. I was still too tough on myself. I decided then and there to learn to 'Be More Gentle with Myself'. Slowly, Softly and Gently were the words that came into my head. I developed some powerful tools to help me recover from burnout. By changing my mindset and using visualisations, meditation and being more gentle with myself I found that by being 'Softer' I actually could become more Powerful.

I went on to create a Softer Success strategy to help individuals and corporate teams learn to prioritise a calm and kind approach leading to smarter and more productive working practices and happier and more fulfilled personal lives. I helped women at work who were feeling overwhelmed and were burning out.

These powerful techniques and tips, based on studies, research and experimentation, are transforming the lives of hundreds of people. My tailor-made program Prevent Burnout, Find Balance enables individual clients and corporate teams to create a more harmonious, peaceful and productive life. The corporate version sets teams and employees up for success by teaching them to become more resilient and to use their energy in a more productive way.

In my workshops and mentoring/coaching sessions I share these tried and tested techniques so that you too can slow down, increase your energy and become more resilient.

CHAPTER 1

You Have Changed

In this chapter, we will investigate how pregnancy changes a woman's brain based on scientific evidence about changes to the brain's structure. Finally, we will examine our hormones and the changes that can happen to the body after pregnancy.

When you have a baby it changes your life big time and I mean really big time. Although, for some of us this can take time to realise. We continue our lives in the same way we did before we had our baby, which of course in some circumstances, can lead to unexpected negative results, such as burnout.

Everything Around You Is Now Different

A study published by *Nature Neuroscience*, December 2016, titled *Pregnancy leads to long lasting changes in human brain structure*, by co-author Elseline Hoekzema, Leiden University, the Netherlands, investigated the effects of pregnancy on the human brain. She and her team studied first-time mothers and fathers, as well as women who had never given birth to a child. Their results indicated that the changes in brain structure, which occurred during pregnancy can remain for up to two years after childbirth.

When communicating with Elseline about this research, she told me that the results indicated that pregnancy dramatically changes the grey matter of a woman's brain, especially in structures that are important for social processes such as empathy and understanding others people's thoughts and emotions. These processes, which are activated when a woman looks at her baby.'

These changes indicate a natural and positive transition into motherhood, helping a woman attach, bond and understand her newborn after birth.

This research can help us to understand why women can feel differently after childbirth and why having a baby is such a big change for most people.

This is a very interesting topic and there is still more research being done on the subject. Elseline Hoekzema received various research grants and is now continuing her research for the Brain and Development Laboratory at the University of Leiden.

My Experience

One moment I was pregnant and the next moment this beautiful baby was in my arms. I felt overwhelmed with unconditional love and my heart was bursting with joy. It was an amazing moment when my baby was born. But as much as I loved my baby, it was also a huge shock when my husband and I came home from the hospital. My wonderful mum was there to help me and I thought I had breastfeeding under control. One evening we put my daughter in her crib, we all had a nice dinner and went to bed. About two hours later, she was awake and crying and I could not get her to stop. Feeding her worked for a little while, but she started crying again. I changed her nappy and cuddled her. Eventually, it hit me; I didn't know what she wanted! I had a huge responsibility for this tiny little being and she couldn't tell me what she needed. I had to work it out. This was a whole new world to me – I was a mum. No matter how prepared you think you are, nothing anyone says or does will prepare you for the emotional rollercoaster of becoming a parent.

My mum was an incredible support during these first few weeks, as well as my husband, but he was working. A few days after we got home, I unintentionally started challenging myself to the limits of my physical and mental capacity. My body was recovering from the birth but I told my mum I wanted to go for a walk. We walked together for about twenty minutes to the shops with the baby in the pushchair. Once we got there, I was out of breath and sweating. My intuition was telling me I had done too much already! My baby was crying, so we found a cafe to sit down where I could breastfeed. Although, I didn't suffer from postnatal depression, I did feel quite low those first few weeks. Was it the baby blues? My energy was low and I overheated every time I took any exercise. I struggled to walk, even for twenty minutes and of course I experienced sleep deprivation.

Thankfully, my amazing friend and birth coach, Tracey-Anne Neill who was also my reflexologist during pregnancy was an incredible support, as were the new mummy friends I made. My birth coach kept in touch and popped by from time to time to see how I was doing. My daughter was not very big, so I needed to feed her a lot, which meant sitting down, frequently. I struggled with breastfeeding and eventually had to supplement my milk because my daughter was not growing enough. It was during this time that my birth coach and dear friend was such a huge support. She helped keep me on track and encouraged me to enjoy the moments with my daughter and look at her and enjoy this newfound love instead.

Nerdy Girl

During the first few months, I was a bit of a 'nerdy girl'; nothing has changed in that department six years down the line! For example, I turned up at the first doctor's appointment with my smart black handbag and no nappies for my baby. When I went out for a walk with my other mummy friends, I sometimes found it hard to balance the pushchair while trying to keep up with my friends and so my poor baby got swung around from left to right!

I didn't understand the changes, which were going on inside me and so I continued living my life in the same way, ignoring my gut and trying to stay perfect and organised within my new crazy baby world. Every day, my baby girl looked immaculate in her pretty, hyper-clean clothes and everyone said how sweet she looked, which made me feel good. But I got super stressed if her clothes were dirty because then things weren't perfect anymore. I tried to keep up my 'good girl' status but was rushing around doing the washing about ten times a day and exhausting myself. This was adding unnecessary pressure to an already demanding new situation for me, on my own at home rather than in a busy office, knowing exactly what was expected of me every day!

On top of that, I didn't recognise my body after childbirth. Nobody told me I would continue to look six months pregnant for many weeks after I gave birth. I had stretch marks, varicose veins and I was not able to walk far without feeling faint, let alone run or jog as I used to enjoy so much!

Some women go through pregnancy and come out the other side looking exactly the same. Other people like me end up with physical scars, a wobbly tummy and stretch marks. Everyone is different. It can take up to eighteen months, or more, for your body to recover from the birth of a baby and that is if you don't become pregnant again in the meantime. Some changes only last for a few weeks; it can take six weeks for your uterus to change back to its pre-pregnancy size, for example, while other changes may last for the long term.

Changes

Research shows that hormonal balance is vital to a healthy mind and body, but can be disrupted in so many ways. Many hormonal fluctuations occur naturally, such as in puberty, menopause and peri-menopause. However, there is plenty of research completed about hormones and how they can affect women when they become pregnant in their 30s or 40s.

It is clear that hormones can play havoc in a woman's world. Never underestimate your hormones. Whether you are going through IVF, have Pre-Menstrual Tension (PMT) or are in the peri-menopausal stage.

During my twenties and thirties, I suffered from mild PMT but it didn't affect my life in the same way it did after having children. After my second daughter was born, I breastfed successfully and once I stopped breastfeeding, my periods came back with a vengeance. I believe that the severe PMT and heavy periods I experienced were a direct contribution to my burnout. It affected my sleep and my daily moods. PMT caused me anxiety and outbursts of anger. It was not until I went through a burnout one year later, when I was forty-one that I started to realise that hormones played such a huge part in my life.

At this time, I made an appointment with a gynaecologist. The first thing he told me when I explained my symptoms was "You are peri-menopausal, welcome to your forties!" I felt like Bridget Jones when she was told she was a geriatric mum at the age of thirty-five! I was shocked and did not feel ready for the menopause. He told me that the Mirena coil could be the solution to my problems. While it may not be for all women, the Mirena coil releases a small amount of progesterone into the uterus. This thins the lining of the womb so periods become lighter. A secondary effect is that it can help reduce PMT for some women. With me, it took three months to show results and my sleeping patterns became better, my periods were less heavy and my PMT was bearable.

We now know that hormones play a huge part in a woman's life. This is even more significant because so many of us are having babies later in life. We are also juggling home life and work and we have more stress to manage in our daily lives than women had previously.

However, London based Professor of Gynaecologist, John Studd, DSc, MD, FRCOG, who I consulted in writing this book believes that common problems, such as depression, PMT or menopausal symptoms are easy and safe to treat with bio-identical hormones.

He researches hormonal imbalances using an in-depth questionnaire, blood tests and a bone density scan. Depending on the outcome, he prescribes oestrogen or testosterone gels, which have less risk than pill-form hormones. His treatments have resulted in positive improvements; women with depression feel more like themselves; PMT symptoms improve and women going through menopause feel much better.

Professor Studd told me that, "As PMT is essentially due to hormone changes that occur after ovulation, the logical way to treat it is to suppress ovulation. This is done naturally of course, with pregnancy or the menopause, but younger women also respond to transdermal oestrogens, which suppress ovulation and can be given by patches or gels. It is possible to include testosterone for women who have poor energy, depression or a poor libido."

According to Professor Studd, 'Libido is an important barometer of relationship hormonal status and mood is an important indicator for PMT, menopause and depression.' So, have some fun and keep check of your libido, ladies!

It is also very hard to be at work when your hormones are fluctuating. If you are pregnant, have PMT or are going through IVF treatment. When I was pregnant, I suffered in silence with a male boss who I knew did not understand what I was going through on a daily basis. This meant that I carried on working to the same gruelling schedule and was not looking after myself properly. But it makes sense that employers actually know what you are going through and why you may behave in a slightly different way to before. Many companies now have Employee Relation Programmes where you can talk to the company doctor or a counsellor.

There are also very effective ways to balance hormones through nutrition and exercise, which we will have a closer look at in Chapter 7.

Case Study: Anne, 44

Anne met her partner in her forties. Quite soon they started trying for a baby. First naturally and then through numerous rounds of failed IVF. By the time she was forty-three years old, she was desperate. Eventually, she went to Spain where they found an egg donor, she became pregnant and had her son at the age of forty-four. An absolute blessing! During her pregnancy, she had some complications and a colleague suggested she went to see the company doctor. The company doctor suggested that Anne worked three days a week on reduced hours and this decision ensured that she felt comfortable with her working schedule and that her boss understood.

Not all companies will do this, but if you can speak to your company doctor or someone in Human Resources Department, it can open doors for you and make all the difference to your pregnancy, as well as your performance at work.

Following childbirth, there are many natural hormonal changes that take place in the body. It is quite common for childbirth to alter hormonal balance and throw you off track, causing all kinds of negative health symptoms. It doesn't always happen after your first baby. It can happen after your second or third, or any time after childbirth. If you suspect your hormones are out of balance, it is well worth having them checked out properly by your doctor.

How to Embrace Change

Now we have investigated the changes pregnancy can have on a women's brain, as well as physical changes to the body and the effect of hormones, it is time to look at how to embrace these changes!

These days many women are having children later in life, when they know who they are within themselves and they are settled in stable relationship and job, a house, and an established social life. The baby arrives and they start to question this new aspect of their lives. 'I feel different' and 'Who am I now?' You are now a mum, but you feel different to how you did pre-baby. How do you find your new identity and adapt to the new you and having a baby in your life?

When my first daughter was born, I loved that my life was enriched with this beautiful little baby. However I continued to think and feel the same way about myself. I told myself my persona had not changed, but in fact, it had. I kept challenging myself to the limits of my physical and mental capacity. For example, when our daughter was six weeks old, my husband and I celebrated our first wedding anniversary. We went out for dinner and, because I was breastfeeding, we took the baby with us. We ended up being able to have only ten minutes of conversation with a drink and that was more or less our dinner. The baby was very unsettled that evening and we took turns to look after her. Although on the one hand, I was glad that I had managed to get out with my husband on that special day, at the time I also felt as if my life was very different because we could no longer go out for dinner in the same way.

One habit that has helped me embrace the change of motherhood is to write down three events or people I am grateful for each day.

It can be something as small as, 'I am grateful for being able to hear my baby laugh' or 'I am grateful for the tickling competition I had with my daughter'. Instead of being annoyed or frustrated with the new situation, it helps me to appreciate the amazing new experiences I'm having. Even on days when I don't feel so positive I write down three points to be grateful for and it changes my mood instantly. Now, I truly believe that having children has enriched my life to no extent but of course, as I am only human, they do totally stress me out sometimes!

Change is inevitable when you have children. In fact, a work colleague told me years ago that, 'the only constant thing in life is change.' Learning to go with the flow is not easy. Changes are constant with new babies.

Another way we can embrace change is to learn from our little ones. This sounds strange but actually our little babies and children can teach us so much. We want to be the best possible mother and a good example for our children. But actually children teach us as much as we teach them. Children show us that we can be ourselves being in the moment and living life to the fullest.

Think about the following three questions and see if they give you a new perspective?

Cara's Three Questions Exercise

- *Why not take a look at yourself through your child's eyes?*
- *Does it feel like you are telling them off all the time?*
- *Would you prefer to dance with them and have fun?*

A bit of both is probably a fair assessment of me as a mum. I tell my kids off, if they are naughty because after all I am a mum and I am trying to guide and teach them, but I also dance and sing with them and have fun. My kids see me laugh at myself because I am a bit of a nerdy mama! I will often hit the dance floor in our kitchen, for a boogie with my kids. My make up will be smudged and I'll lose my slippers, but we have fun! When they were babies, I did the same thing, but they got covered in milk because my vigorous dancing caused them to regurgitate, the poor mites!

Why is dancing good for you? Research shows that physical movement such as dancing releases endorphins, the chemicals in your brain that can help you feel good. Studies show that a little physical activity every day can help kids concentrate better and this will boost their learning abilities. Remembering dance steps and focusing on rhythm is a great exercise for your brain. Sometimes, when you get older, the part of your brain that controls learning and memory shrinks. Research shows that physical activity such as dancing may help stop that happening or slow it down. Need I say more?

Above all, it is simply pure fun! So, ladies get your dancing shoes on; it works wonders for everyone!

My hubby and I regularly have a boogie on the dance floor too, yes once again in our kitchen! Sometimes, we simply jump up and down like the kids. My advice is to get fun and playful and remember to laugh at yourself.

Also, it is very important to make time for your partner. It is very tiring to have a small baby or young children in your lives and sometimes you simply want to collapse on the sofa at the end of the day. However, having five or ten minutes of laughing and fun together or time chatting with your partner is so very important. It does not have to be long, but it is a powerful form of connecting. I often write down how grateful I am for my partner. He is an amazing support. It also helps in the moments when I get annoyed, which does happen because I am only human!

Here is a personal and true example of one of the things I am grateful for.

"I am grateful for my wonderful husband because he helped get the kids into bed tonight so that I could relax."

Insights

Think of three people or events you are grateful for during your day. Write them down and read it out loud to yourself. You will be surprised with what you come up with!

Practical Tips

1. Laugh!

- When things don't go as you had planned them – smile, shrug your shoulders and laugh at yourself or tell a friend – it will help you let it go!
- Watch comedy; a dose of a comedian show does wonders for me when I need a good laugh.
- Join in when your kids are having fun – laugh and play with them – even if you are hopeless at somersaults, like me!

2. Dance; wherever you can, squeeze in a boogie!

- Remembering dance steps and focusing on rhythm is a great exercise for your brain.
- It is soul food; above all forms of exercise, dancing releases the most endorphins.
- It is simply pure fun!

3. Ask your doctor to check your hormone levels and understand what they mean

- How do you feel before, during and after your period?
- Write it down and chart it.
- If you think you have mood swings and you are struggling with them, talk about it with your doctor.

CHAPTER 2

Talk to Other People

In this chapter, we will explore mental health and examine parental guilt. Finally, we will investigate why it is important to ask for help and talk to other people about how you feel.

Open Up About Mental Health

There remains a massive taboo around mental health. There is a frequently quoted statistic from the World Health Organisation that one in four of us will suffer from a mental health problem each year. But why is it so rarely spoken about? And what does it mean for the sufferers, especially in the workplace?

Mental health is as important as physical health. As a society, we are more open about our physical problems with little worry of rejection and prejudice. Why isn't it that way with mental health?

When I went through my burnout at work, I felt ashamed and embarrassed to talk to people about it. Then I joined a parent community committee at work and I started to feel more confident talking about my burnout and I started to help other parents so they could feel more confident about opening up too.

Going back to statistics if every one in four people suffer from some form of mental health condition each year, then I believe that we need to speak up about it much more.

Fortunately, in 2013, all members of the World Health Assembly adopted the Comprehensive Mental Health Action Plan. This plan, with a clear vision, objectives and targets is the highest political commitment that mental health has received to date. The plan includes a variety of actions to decrease stigma around mental disorders and the discrimination faced by people with mental disorders and their families. The World Health Organisation is assisting countries to implement the Action Plan during 2013 – 2020.

This plan recommends that all countries prioritise investment in mental health services regardless of their wealth levels. In addition, they have implemented strategies to promote positive mental health in the workplace; As a result, The World Health Organisation's Global Plan of Action on Worker's Health 2008 – 2017, has assisted organisations and workers. Also, they produced a series of booklets called, *Protecting Workers Health*, which provides guidance on common issues, such as harassment and stress that can affect the health of workers and include access to occupational health services.

Research shows that many more companies and workplaces are now putting systems in place to help employees. This can be in the form of an Employee Assistance Programme. For example, the company I worked for during my burnout offered on site counselling. There was also a service offered internally called 'parent gurus'. These 'gurus' were other parents in the company who offered an hour of their time to speak to fellow employees about anything they needed help or advice with.

We are being given excellent leadership from the British Royal Family who support mental health via the *Heads Together* campaign in the United Kingdom, which is a partnership with experienced and inspiring charities that provide frontline mental health support to people who may need it. The *Heads Together* campaign combines charities with many years of experience who aim to raise awareness and tackle the stigma around mental health in the United Kingdom.

Let's get rid of that taboo around mental health!

Case Study: Irene, 31

When Irene called in sick to her work with a bad chest infection, she received numerous 'get well cards and emails' and people kept asking her how she was feeling. A few months later, Irene was signed off work for stress. She didn't hear anything from her colleagues during the whole time she was away. Unfortunately, too many managers or colleagues don't really know what to say or how to approach it when someone is signed off work for stress or mental health. It is often not spoken about, but this needs to change.

Guilt

In a recent survey by United Kingdom-based baby care product company NUK they discovered that 87 percent of mothers feel guilty at some point.

All the mothers I spoke with while researching for this book, told me they often feel guilty. Ladies please listen. It is time to stop feeling guilty. Why do women feel guilty when they leave their children, either to go back to work or because they need a break?

The key triggers for parental guilt resulting from the NUK survey were:

- being too busy or tired to give their child what they need;
- not being able to afford everything they want for their child and
- returning to work too soon after giving birth.

It is claimed that these triggers can make parents feel guilty, plus there is the idealist image of 'perfect parenting' bombarding us from a variety of media outlets. However, there is actually no 'perfect parenting guide' because each family is unique. What works for one family may not work for another family. My advice to you is to find a way that works for you and your family unit. Never beat yourself up about it. After all, it is impossible to be a perfect parent!

For example, parenting now is very different from what it was in my mother's generation forty or fifty years ago. There was less influence from the media and to a certain extent, the children were allowed to get on with it. My mum often tells me that she was not as involved or did not analyse her children or how to parent as much as our generation does. Her advice is simple but profound. "Let it go, you can only do your best as a parent and we all make mistakes." Remember that we all learn to be a parent as we do it and this continues all our lives.

When I went back to work after giving birth to my first daughter, I remember thinking there were so many balls to juggle and I wanted to juggle them all myself. I wanted to be a perfect wife for my husband with dinner waiting for him when he got back from work; a caring and loving mummy; a good friend; a good sister and daughter and also, do well at my job and try to find time to exercise and do all the things I enjoyed as well! These were too many balls to juggle and when I got pregnant the second time around, my body started telling me something serious! Slow down, slow down, slow down. But I continued at the same pace until I ended up in hospital with bleeding and swollen feet. The doctors told me it was time to finish at work and take it easy.

I felt guilty that I was not able to handle it all because we women can do it all right? I was convinced that I could do everything at the same time. But in reality, it was actually okay to ask for help.

Being a parent is a natural human function and it is not meant to be as hard as some people find it. Actually, we are not meant to parent alone. Humans are social animals. It is more natural that humans need help from other family members such as grandmothers, aunts, uncles etc.

Many studies by social scientists and anthropologists throughout history have found that we were meant to raise children in small family groups. Where parenting takes place in a group setting with support for the parents, as well as the children, the children also benefit because they also begin to take care of their brothers and sisters.

A few years ago, I spent time volunteering for a charity and helped build houses for children orphaned by AIDS in South Africa. It was very special to get to know the local families. They all supported each other and the grandmas stepped in for the mums or dads and the sisters helped each other out. My own situation is not like that because both my husband's family and my family live in another country. We have learned to depend on each other instead and our friends and local help. This is a modern type of family group.

Think about the five balls of life speech given by former Coca Cola CEO, Brian Dyson. Imagine life is a game in which you are juggling five balls. The balls are called work, family, health, friends and integrity and you are keeping all of them in the air. But one day you finally come to understand that work is a rubber ball. If you drop it, it will bounce back. The other four balls are made of glass. If you drop one of these, it will be scuffed, nicked, perhaps even shattered. Remember ladies. Your family, health, friends and integrity are critically important.

Nerdy Girl

When I went through my burnout, I started taking yoga classes. I practised yoga all the time, including when I was playing with my children. One day my oldest daughter – then three years old – asked what I was doing. I told her that I was practising yoga. She asked if she could do it with me. We both lay down on the yoga mat. We did the 'happy baby' pose, which my daughter took literally. She thought that this pose meant she had to laugh like a baby. My darling daughter started laughing and didn't stop – maybe it was because I looked so funny doing the pose – however, then we all started laughing and had so much fun! 'Happy baby pose' in our house is now a call to laugh!

Also, in an attempt to juggle it all, I dropped off my dry cleaning one day and completely forgot to pick it up until one day my husband came home with my dry cleaning. He had bumped into the shop owner who had asked him if I was okay because I had not picked up my dry cleaning for weeks!

Cara's Three Questions Exercise

- *Can you practice scrapping something off your 'to do' list instead of adding to it?*
- *Can you think of someone you can ask to help you out today so you can have a break?*
- *Can you let go of your parental guilt by explaining to yourself that you are constantly learning?*

Now, we have looked at mental health and parental guilt, as well as juggling all the balls of life, it is time to explore how to share your feelings.

How to Share Your Feelings

Once my second daughter was born, we moved house to an area with good schools and a more suitable environment. But I found it hard to settle in. I was questioning who I was. I went back to work and I thought that would help stabilise me; in fact it did the opposite. Unknowingly again, I challenged myself and my physical and mental capacity. I kept going although inside I was unsure I was doing the right thing and felt stressed coping with work and two young children. I felt I needed to keep up 'appearances' because all of the mums around me seemed to be coping brilliantly with work and kids. On hindsight, I wish I had opened up to them and also to my husband. I was heading towards a burnout but did not realise it. I kept all of my feelings inside and did not really know how to express myself.

It is always important to talk to other people about how you feel. Start by talking to someone you trust for example a friend or your partner. If you feel uncomfortable or embarrassed, then your local Medical Centre may have counselling on offer or companies may offer an Employee Assistance Programme. Over the past few years, I have learned to share my feelings and talk openly about burnout, anxiety and insomnia. Talking really helps. I have found that explaining what has happened to me helps other people open up and share their feelings too. Slowly, I started helping other people who were going through a similar situation. I signed up as a 'parent guru' at work and started helping my colleagues who were feeling stressed and anxious. I really enjoyed helping other people and it helped me realise that I had a calling to do this.

It may feel uncomfortable at first and I certainly felt uncomfortable talking about my feelings in the first instance. I also remember wishing I could speak with someone who had gone through a burnout too.

Insights

My advice to you is…let it out. It is always better to let things out than keeping them in…well, maybe not literally!

Nicola Bird at *Little Piece of Mind* holds regular webinars on anxiety. I completed one of her courses online and it positively shifted my mindset. As a result, I consulted her when writing this book. She told me that her method is extremely powerful and once it 'clicks' it can be a game changer to free you from your anxiety. I highly recommend Nicola's webinars and have referenced them at the end of this book.

Practical Tips

1. Open up!

- Talk to a friend, colleague or professional who you trust.

2. Work on yourself

- Answer the following questions, writing down how you feel in detail on a piece of paper or in a lovely, fresh new journal.
  - What you are feeling now?
  - What would you like to change?
  - How will you feel when you have achieved this change?

3. Take action!

- Now, tear out your piece of paper and burn it in the fire to let go of your feelings and move on!

CHAPTER 3

Stop Fighting

In this chapter, we will investigate how pushing yourself to the limits of your capacity does not benefit anyone and can lead to overwhelm and burnout. I describe my own personal experiences with burnout and explore the impacts of social media. Finally, we will explore tips on how to prevent burnout.

That Overwhelm Feeling

Do you feel like there are too many things to do every day? That life keeps getting busier? Do you feel overwhelmed in your life?

We are often stuck in 'doing' mode without taking time to recover and rebalance. We are stressed, struggling to deal with the ever-growing demands of both our work and our personal lives.

In Susan Scott's book, *The Young Professionals Guide On How To Prevent Burnout*, she states that digital technology means we are now accessible 24/7 so the boundaries between our work and our personal lives have become blurred. But we also want it all, a great job, lovely home, fit body, fulfilling hobbies, happy family and so we push ourselves constantly to achieve more. But if we keep pushing ourselves this can lead to overwhelm and eventually to burnout.

Susan Scott's definition of burnout is: 'A state of emotional, physical and mental exhaustion'. It is caused by excessive and prolonged stress. It occurs when you feel overwhelmed and unable to meet constant demands.

I consulted Susan while writing this book and she said 'the more we can spread the word about burnout, the more aware people will become of it'.

Burnout is a gradual process. The signs and symptoms are subtle at first, but they get worse as time goes on.

While researching this book many women I talked to about burnout had experienced some sort of 'paralysis'. They felt so overwhelmed that they were no longer able to do even the smallest task. I will explain more about my own experiences with this in 'the hamster wheel'.

Well, the good news is that it doesn't have to get to that point. You can do something about it and prevent it in the first place and I will give you helpful tips about this, at the end of this chapter.

My Experience

As I have mentioned, during my burnout, I started suffering from insomnia; actually I think this had sneaked into my life once my first daughter was born and I went back to a stressful job. I struggled to get to sleep and woke up at 5am every morning; it felt like Ground Hog Day! I was desperate to 'solve' it and one day I was talking about insomnia to a personal trainer at my local gym. He told me he had suffered night terrors and recommended a wonderful sleep and energy expert. Her name was Dr Nerina Ramlakhan and she taught me that sleep can actually reflect what is going on in your life. Given the fact I was going through a burnout, it was hardly surprising that my sleep took the first hit. Nerina encouraged me to take a different approach to sleep. I learned to 're-name' it and call it 'rest'. I learned that I could not 'control' sleep. I learned many amazing techniques from Nerina when I found it hard to settle down at night but also when I felt anxious during the day. For example, using yoga poses and breathing as well as eating something within 30 minutes of waking up. I soon noticed an improvement. However, the most important thing I now know about sleep is to simply let it be. You can't control it in any way.

Interestingly, Roger Ekirch author of *Day's Close: Night in Times Past*, October 2006, a scientist and historian at Virginia Tech University USA discovered the concept of segmented sleep. His research found that before the Industrial Revolution, humans slept in two separate segments at night. He discovered that people went to bed when it got dark at 8 or 9pm and woke up again around midnight. This was the time that most people used to have something to eat, meditate, pray or have sex. Then, they went back to sleep until the early hours of the morning. With the coming of artificial light and the Industrial Revolution, people started living on a time ordered schedule and slept in one long stretch. But it can help put things in perspective when you wake up in the middle of night, to remember the fact that humans historically did not always sleep in one long stretch. They followed nature's rhythm of night and day.

Social Media

A report published by the Next Web in August 2017, demonstrated that the number of people using social media around the world had passed the three billion mark – that is around 40% of the world's population. Growth trends show no signs of slowing either, with suggestions that the number of active social media users is growing at a rate of one million new users per day. It is claimed by many reports that we are spending more than two hours a day on our social media platforms. Many businesses have formed meaningful relationships through the power of social media. It is an amazing new way of marketing. This is positive and hugely helpful.

But does social media create stress for individuals?

In a BBC article, *Is social media bad for you?* January 2018, it stated that because social media is relatively new, it is hard to find conclusive evidence. Research that does exist relies on self-reporting, which can be flawed. However, this is a fast growing area of research and many clues are beginning to show that social media is creating stress for some individuals.

One of the chief contributors to social media related stress is our tendency to compare ourselves to other people. We receive constant updates from friends or family showing how 'perfect' their life is, and this can cause feelings of inadequacy. It can also cause social media users to become anxious or stressed because they worry that life isn't as exciting or that they haven't accomplished as much as their peers. This can create pressure to find ways to present an idealised version of their own life that doesn't reflect reality.

Sometimes stress can be caused by idealised versions of social media, exposure to stressful news and events through social media, which can also increase personal feelings of anxiety.

Social media provides constant updates. This motivates people to continually check their status and newsfeed on mobile devices. Many people feel a constant need to check their social media. They only feel better when they have turned off their mobile device. So, the question for all of us is; how can we limit stress from social media?

Case Study: Janine, 36

After feeling she was constantly comparing herself to her friends on social media, Janine decided to test how it felt if she quit social media. She disconnected from all social media, apart from WhatsApp, which kept her in touch with her family and friends. The feeling she had when she disconnected from social media was amazing. Janine felt liberated and free. Once she stopped checking social media she realised how much more time she had and her friends stayed in touch via WhatsApp or email instead. After one year, she went back onto social media but limited the time she used it per day.

Cara's Three Questions Exercise

- *Are you able to limit your time on social media?*
- *Can you put your phone or tablet away as much as possible when you are with your partner or family?*
- *Are you able to simple 'be' and enjoy valuable time with family and friends without checking your phone?*

My advice is to stop trying to keep up. It is okay not to follow everything on social media.

The Hamster Wheel

After the birth of my second daughter, I started to feel anxious that there were so many things I needed to do. With two children under the age of three, fluctuating hormones and working a four day week at full throttle, which in reality meant five days, it all started to take its toll. When I had been back at work for about four months after my maternity leave, I started to feel like a hamster on a treadmill. I could not get out and there were so many things to do I could not stop running.

Looking back, I can see this is a classic example of my perfectionism. I couldn't let anything go or delegate. What I didn't realise was that I was actually in control of the hamster wheel and I could slow down and simply be; a revelation!

Once I got to the point of burnout, it was very difficult to do anything. Any little job seemed like a mountain, from the simplest tasks at work such as attending meetings or giving the children a bath, making dinner or reading a book. My mind was on overdrive and it needed to calm down. I started to look at ways to quieten my mind. I looked into meditation and mindfulness. But I was convinced this was some kind of new age fad and couldn't see how would it help me. But at that point, I was happy to try anything. I found an amazing App called Calm and started to meditate for ten minutes every day, focusing on my breathing. It made a huge difference! I now regularly meditate and practice mindfulness.

Why meditation?

I discovered that meditation and breathing can help reduce stress and can uplift your mood. Meditation and breathing can increase lung capacity and helps the body receive more oxygen. Meditation can help to settle our mind and calm us so we can focus on what we are doing. We gain awareness of what is in our minds and we can identify our negative thoughts. It is healthy to realise that our thoughts are not who we are. This will help us become less identified with our negative thoughts so they start to lose their power. Meditation can also help you cultivate compassion for yourself and other people. There are many other benefits to meditation that you will discover when you try it for yourself.

Nerdy Girl

I remember one funny situation to do with meditation when I was in a bit of a rush one day. I started to cook soup for my kids. While stirring vigorously – I don't know why I did that – I ended up spilling soup on my tummy. It felt sore so I put a packet of frozen peas on it. Then, I promptly realised it was school pick up time and dashed out to collect the kids, with the frozen peas still tucked into the front of my tights! None of the mums on the school run noticed my big tummy, thank goodness. When I got home with the kids I took my coat off and realised that the frozen peas were still on my tummy. When I took out the frozen peas my oldest daughter was watching me and asked me 'Mama, where you trying to cook the peas on your tummy?'

How to Let Go to Prevent Burnout

Now we have looked at overwhelm and social media as well as the Hamster Wheel, it is time to take a look at how to let go and prevent burnout. I will show you that you can stop running on that Hamster Wheel and simply 'be'.

I have also described many of the benefits of meditation and mindfulness. They are powerful tools and can assist you when trying to slow down your racing mind.

When I went back to work after my second daughter was born, I started to experience overwhelm and was running faster and faster on the Hamster Wheel. I placed a high value on checking off my 'to do' list and answering all my emails straight away.

Often, we are led to believe that success depends on our ability to accomplish more in less time and if we are not 'pushing' ourselves then we are not going to get where we want. No wonder that many people feel stressed when they can't keep up or get ahead.

In my case, I thought that if I ran faster on the Hamster Wheel, ticking off my "to do" list and doing everything quicker, I would get it all done. The Hamster Wheel had to keep spinning.

I was so wrong.

What if...you actually start on the Hamster Wheel with the intention of simply 'being' and you put your trust in the fact that wherever you are in its cycle is exactly where you need to be. You could slow down to a more natural rhythm whether this means you are; walking, jogging or standing absolutely, completely still. Static. Nothing would really happen, right?

Stand still on that Hamster Wheel, ladies! Take time to 'be'. Sit down on the sofa and look out of the window... for hours if you need to. Daydream. Breathe. Do nothing.

Once you can stand still on the Hamster Wheel, you are also able to climb off. This can help you take a step back and take a balanced look at your life. It will help you slow down and can get a clearer idea of what you are need to do differently to change your life. In my workshops I facilitate a session about 'how to get off the Hamster wheel'. It is very powerful and I have found it has helped countless women – and men – to take a step back and look at what it is they need to change in their lives to become more gentle with themselves.

Try the following visualisation. When practiced frequently, it can become a powerful tool to help you let go and quieten your mind.

- Imagine you are holding several balloons.
- They represent all your worries and concerns.
- Now, visualise letting them go, one by one.
- They are up in the sky floating around, but you are not holding on to them, anymore.

Insights

When you notice you are feeling overwhelmed, anxious or stressed, start doing meditation, take care of your diet and limit your intake of alcohol and caffeine. I am not a nutritionist, however I have experienced these benefits first hand.

Practical Tips

1. Manage your social media usage

- Reduce the time you spend on social media by turning your phone off one hour before going to bed.

2. Meditate and be mindful

- Download a meditation app, such as Calm or Insight Timer and start with 10 minutes a day.

3. Sleep naturally

- Never worry if you have trouble sleeping. Instead, focus on resting.

Stop Fighting

CHAPTER 4

Take Time for Yourself

In this chapter we will explore why it is important to breathe, slow down and find time for yourself. I describe my own experiences with connecting to nature and being mindful. Finally, we explore how we can connect to something bigger and prioritise what is important.

Breathe

Time for yourself is so important. For most mums it is rare time because with children, work and life in general, we can become very busy. We often put ourselves last on the list. However, I cannot stress enough the importance of taking time out to breathe, meditate and connect with nature.

During my recovery, I was advised to concentrate on my breathing. Deep breathing can release stress and provide many health benefits, such as feeling more focused and relaxed.

Additional benefits of deep breathing include reduction in stress and blood pressure; strengthening of abdominal and intestinal muscles and general body aches and pains. Deep breathing also promotes better blood flow, releases toxins from the body and aids in healthy sleep. These benefits result in increased energy levels. It is important to breathe deeply and often. Once you get into the swing of it, it feels great!

Once I started to practice deep breathing, I realised that I did not know how to do it! I ended up feeling more short of breath. I was recommended to practise yoga positions and elevate my legs. This really helped and I could feel that I was breathing more deeply. Ladies; take a few minutes several times a day to concentrate on your breathing.

Cara's Three Question Exercise

- *Can you practise a simple two-minute breathing exercise?*
- *Can you schedule fifteen minutes in the day that you devote to yourself for 'me time'?*
- *How often are you able to do what you feel like doing, not what you think you should be doing?*

I have highlighted how meditation can help, but now we are going to look at the importance of connecting to nature.

Connecting to Nature

Why is it important to connect to nature? Everyday life can be noisy; cars, planes, traffic, banging, drilling and other people's voices. We also spend a lot of time using technology inside buildings. Connecting with nature and being outside can help you find peace in your busy life. Spend time each day outside observing what is happening around you. You will begin to notice things about your environment that you have not seen before. You will increase awareness of your surroundings.

You can go for a walk. For example, for me it is about a ten minute walk to my children's school. I often have a mindful walk where I listen to the birds, take in the colours of the trees and look around. It doesn't matter if you walk in a local park or around your neighbourhood. Getting outside exposure and exercising are good for your health and strengthen your connection with nature. Fresh air is so important!

There was a time when all I was doing was going to work and commuting on the underground train twice a day. I was either in an office building or taking public transport and, by the time I got home, it was dark. I began to crave nature, like you crave a certain food. My soul was in need of 'green'.

I decided to start gardening. Yes ladies, gardening! It is not for all of us, but it fits with me. We all know that flowers can make you feel great and there is also a plethora of evidence that gardening can be good for you too!

A 2015 poll by the online gardening company Bakker.com discovered that 88 percent of people stated mental wellbeing as a reason for heading out into the garden. People find that the fresh air and a sense of achievement helps them balance their mental wellbeing! You can get your hands dirty and nurture growing life. But if gardening is not for you, then appreciating a garden with family and friends is also good for your health.

Case Study: Rebecca, 28

Rebecca suffered from a burnout when she had a high-powered job working for a large corporation. She recovered when she left the job to start a family. She had two delightful children and decided to work part-time from home. During this time, she suffered a second mini burnout. Rebecca realised that she had to change things in her life and started meditation. At the same time, she got a dog because she felt the need to be outside more often and a dog seemed the perfect way to make sure she had regular walks in nature. Now, Rebecca is outside walking for at least one hour a day and she feels so much better for it, physically as well as mentally and emotionally.

Me Time

The combination of our caregiving duties at home and the responsibilities of work can cause us to neglect our own basic needs. When we neglect our own wellbeing we can become overwhelmed and energy depleted. We all want to be generous, but true caregiving includes tending to our own needs as well as those we care for. The Calm app reminds us that mindful caregiving means being aware of our strengths, weaknesses, motivations and needs. It means providing care that is effective, but also sustainable. If caring for other people leaves us exhausted, we need to ask ourselves; 'Am I doing too much?' and 'Am I taking on too much responsibility?'

For example, a flight attendant directs the passengers to put their own oxygen masks on before helping other people, in the case of an emergency. Think about it. We need to top up our own reserves before helping other people. I highly suggest you try: meditation; exercise; a long bath; or a quiet afternoon on your own.

Remember, your first duty of care is always to yourself.

Being Peacefully Busy

We spend much of our time rushing around being busy, but what if we change this to being 'peacefully busy'. What does that look like? Would 'peacefully busy' help you balance work and life? Would 'peacefully busy' mean you prioritise 'me time' first? For example, would your day be planned around a mindful walk outside noticing the trees and twenty minutes of meditation? I know life is hectic and we are all busy, but lovely ladies, please plan these activities into your schedule first and your day will be so much more peaceful. Of course, we are only human and sometimes you may simply have a 'bad day'! Think about it. When someone asks you how you are, how might you feel if you said, 'I'm peacefully busy'? Does it actually make you feel less rushed?

Being too busy is killing us. Too many people are suffering from stress and anxiety because of the need to be 'busy' when maybe we need to say 'no' sometimes.

Replace the phrase, 'I'm very busy' or 'I'm too busy' with 'I'm peacefully busy'. How does this make you feel? Does this mean pushing back and saying, "no"? In my case, it does because sometimes I have too much going on and I actually can't do everything.

We tend to value busy people. It may be hard for us to stop using the word 'busy' but 'peacefully busy' resonates more with calm and feels nurturing. It means, 'Yes, I'm busy, but I'm being gentle with myself and looking after myself. I'm taking time out to do the things I need to nurture myself and the things I love so I feel less stressed.'

Ladies! When you wake up in the morning visualise the words "peacefully busy" as your words for the day. They are a golden colour, nurturing and healing. It's a way of being kinder to yourself and other people. It's 'peacefully…busy'.

I have practised being peacefully busy and the positive benefits first hand. When I first started writing this book, I was in a very busy job at a global technology company. I was telling everyone how 'busy' I was. When I left my job, I attended a workshop where I met twelve wonderful women. I had all these lovely projects already on the go, but I realised after speaking with these wonderful women that I could take it one step at a time…and be peacefully busy.

Nerdy Girl

We all need more humour in our lives. I remember one day, I decided to draw a funny face on all the bananas we had in the house. I took them with me for the kids as a snack. My girls could not stop laughing and wanted to make more funny faces on the bananas, it was such a lovely moment!

I try not to take myself too seriously if I can…. and have always loved telling jokes. I love to entertain other people and make them laugh. But when I went through my burnout, it was harder for me to do this. I lost the appetite for it and probably my self-confidence. But my kids helped me bring this into perspective. For example, one Sunday afternoon, I decided to bake a cake from a recipe I had seen in a magazine. Now, I am not really a cake baker but I felt so happy and excited to start baking the cake and enlisted the help of my kids. My little darlings were one and three years old at the time and most of their help consisted of licking the bowl. We had a lot of fun, but slowly I saw that I had made a mistake somewhere and the cake wasn't turning out well. It had a big hole in the middle and the chocolate icing was too runny. When I put the icing on top of the cake, it fell through the hole. My kids thought it was hilarious and renamed the cake 'hole cake with runny icing'. My oldest child kept giggling and saying 'Mama is funny, Mama is funny'. I had chocolate icing on my nose and a 'hole cake with runny icing'! I suddenly got it – the cake was not perfect and actually it was better because it was not perfect. We would not have had as much fun otherwise. I loved it when my kids laughed at this new game! We took pictures and sent them to the family and the 'hole cake with runny icing' made other people chuckle too!

Connect to Something Bigger than Yourself

After years at a global tech company working as an Executive Assistant, I started to wonder what other jobs were out there for me. When I went back to work after my burnout, I felt there was a strong pull to help other people. I didn't want any of my colleagues going through the same thing that I did, so I started helping them.

There is plenty of social research proving that we are all trying to find a deeper meaning in our lives. Scientific research shows that connecting to something bigger than ourselves delivers huge benefits for our wellbeing. This search for meaning can be found through friends, family, children, jobs, but for some people this can also be from meditation, prayer and reflection. It can be through religion, God, Buddha, the Divine or it may be worshipping something in nature.

Take a moment to reflect about whether or not you already do this and if so, write down how you connect to something bigger? You may already be doing this without realising, but if you are not, then think about what can help you feel more at peace? What supports you? It is also worth thinking about which activities, people and beliefs bring us the strongest purpose and passion in our lives. Then, you can focus on making sure you prioritise these areas in your life.

Ladies, take a few minutes to think what is really important to you. Write it down and put it in a place where you can be reminded every day; even on busy days when you are tired and grumpy. Stick you priorities up on the fridge, in the bathroom, your bedroom, your study. Wherever you will see it daily.

For me, becoming a mother changed things drastically. My family, my partner and children and of course, our wonderful friends and family are what is really important to me. But I came here to discover another calling, which is to help other women like YOU and this is the reason for this book.

Insights

Learning to breathe, meditate and connect to nature were three huge contributors to my recovery from burnout; living in a major metropolis and having a busy job took over my life and I lost my connection to nature.

Practical Tips

1. Breathe deeply

- Close your eyes and take a few deep breaths. Notice how you are breathing... and if your breath goes through your nose, lungs and down to your stomach.
- If you have trouble with breathing deeply, check out YouTube for 'how to learn to breathe correctly'.

2. Go outside!

- Hug a tree, really! Well, okay only if you feel like it!
- Go into a garden or park.
- Go for a walk.

3. Take action

- Write down what means the most to you in your life and put it where you will see it every day.

CHAPTER 5

Pretty Lady

In this chapter we investigate how to find your inner beauty, as well as how to take better care of yourself. We will explore the benefits of smiling and laughing. Finally, we will look at beauty through our children's eyes.

Be Glamorous

One of my grandmother's sayings was, 'Never let yourself go darling!' My grandmother, Peggie always looked the part with a fresh clean skirt or dress and sometimes a hat to top it off! She always wore make up and only when she had her make up on did she kiss me again in the morning and say 'Good morning, properly darling'. I loved the fact that my grandmother took such care of herself. She was like that even when she had her children. We live in such different times now, but it is important to look after yourself. It seems as if we have less and less time, but it only takes a minute to slick on some lipstick or lip gloss before you leave the house or make sure your hair is brushed and looks neat.

For example I love wearing dresses and skirts. They make me feel feminine and pretty. Even when my babies were little I wore dresses and felt great – albeit with more kilos than I wanted – but I learnt not to think about the fat rolls! I knew I could wash the dresses when I got baby food on them because most modern washing machines have a quick twenty minute short wash.

Why not start with a new lip gloss or lipstick? Or be playful and find something sexy to wear underneath your clothes; don't worry if you have leaking breasts or have wobbly bits, wearing nice underwear will make you feel much better!

Now don't get me wrong. We all need our pyjama days. But when you make an effort every day it can really make you feel better. You can trick your mind into feeling better!

Obviously, it is important to look after ourselves from the outside, but it is equally as important to look after yourself from the inside, too!

Find Your Inner Beauty

Do you know that feeling when you feel so good about yourself you are bursting with joy? This is your inner beauty coming out! It can be for whatever reason works for you; you may have been to the gym; helped a good friend; have worn something new; had a relaxing bath or had sex! It can make you glow! You don't have to be young; inner beauty can come out at any age! It is important to feel good about yourself and allow your inner beauty to shine.

If you feel good about your body, you feel good about yourself. And if you feel good about your body, you are more inclined to look after it better, to dress it nicely and enjoy it. For example, for years, I struggled with my weight. When I was young, I had puppy fat and a round face. This lasted well into my twenties and I really didn't like my round face and big body. Then, I joined a gym. I had always been into sports at school and I played hockey in my twenties, but one day I decided to up the exercise a notch. I started with step classes. After the class I came out feeling happy, but exhausted. As time went on I became more fit. The best thing was the feeling I got after the class with all those endorphins flooding around! I started to feel better about my body and as a result I started to eat less and lose weight. I remember one day a fellow student told me, 'wow you are looking great'! I had the same face and hair and spots too at the time, but I felt happy about myself and my body and it showed to other people!

Then pregnancy came along and my body changed again.

Ladies, I know how hard it is when your body has changed during pregnancy. These days I have wonderful marks and scars on my body that are the result of two pregnancies, but I don't care. Well, let's be honest, some days I do care, but then I look at my beautiful kids and tell myself I am beautiful and it is all forgotten.

Also, it is important to exercise. Even if you can walk for fifteen minutes a day, it's a good start. Sometimes fifteen minutes is all I can manage! Please hang on in there mamas, you will feel better about your body, but maybe not straight after childbirth or even six months after. But you can learn to accept and love your beautiful changed body.

The actress Sharon Stone has publicly told us she actually locked herself in her bathroom with a bottle of wine. She did not let herself out until she could look at her forty year old face and body with acceptance and love. Now, I'm not saying we should lock ourselves in the bathroom with a bottle of wine, but we can learn to accept ourselves exactly as we are. This is actually really important for our overall wellbeing, inside and out!

Cara's Three Question Exercise

- *Can you look at yourself in the mirror and tell yourself you are beautiful, every day?*
- *Can you accept your body as it is now?*
- *If you are unhappy with your body, what do you want to change?*

I know this may sound ridiculous, but if you tell yourself you are beautiful every day in the mirror you will trick your mind into believing it. Even if you don't feel it at first.

Read, Regina Thomashauer's book about inner glow, *Mama Gena's School of Womanly Arts*.

She believes that glow comes from internal approval not disapproval. She says that to have 'glow' it is important to have 'fun' and I have to agree with her! In Regina's book she states that fun can also mean looking after yourself and nourishing yourself. For example, it could be trying on new clothes or going to a museum on your own or having a massage. We often feel guilty doing things for ourselves, but actually we can embrace these precious moments and make them fun.

Fun can also mean connecting with your inner child, that eight year old who is still living inside us all. Jump in puddles, skip, go out dancing, listen to your favourite upbeat music. Or if you are like me …walk to the top of a big hill and shout 'the hills are alive with the sound of music'! Life can be stressful and sometimes we all need an outlet and the chance to feel like a child again! It will put a spring in your step! There is nothing like a good dose of pure fun to bring out your inner beauty!

Pretty Lady

Now we have looked at having fun, we will explore more ways to find your inner beauty.

When I was young, my grandmother told me to 'smile' and 'stand up straight'. At the time I didn't like it, but now I am eternally grateful because I have learned to stand with a straight back. Standing up straight helps you look taller – and slimmer – and it also helps with our confidence. For many years, research has shown that good posture is linked to better memory, more energy and increased confidence. Good posture can reduce back and neck pain because slouching puts more stress on your back and neck muscles. It can put more stress on the spine. Why not stand up straight, right now? You will notice the benefits straight away!

Amy Cuddy in her October 2012 Ted Talk, 'Your body language may shape who you are' suggested that we can change other people's perceptions and our own body chemistry by changing body positions. Amy, a social psychologist, has researched body language and discovered that how we use our bodies can change our thoughts? She suggests that tiny tweaks can lead to big changes. For example, she recommends that by adopting a two minute power pose you can change your hormone levels. It can increase your testosterone (dominance hormone) and lower your cortisol (stress hormone) levels. This means you have more presence and confidence in a stressful situation, for example a job or media interview.

Smiling and Laughing

Someone who is smiling and happy is like a magnet to attract other happy smiling people. Happy people attract happy people. They convey happiness to other people.

Isn't it amazing how many people look serious? Living in a busy metropolis like London most people do not interact or smile at each other. One day I decided to experiment with this. As I was walking down the street to catch the underground to go to work, I started smiling at people walking past. Some people did not look up, but when I managed to make eye contact – and yes, I was flirting with some of them – but they smiled back! And I hope this cheered up their day as it did mine.

My parent's generation had a lot of fun. My dad is renowned for his joke telling and so are my uncle and aunt. My partner is always joking about things too. I have been lucky enough to inherit this love of telling a joke or funny story. The best part is when you can get people to laugh and enjoy it and that makes me laugh too! I want to emphasise how important it is to laugh and smile. It helps us go through life with a lighter note. Smile, laugh, or listen to a joke; maybe tell one yourself. It can alleviate your mood in difficult times. Go and do it yourself today. Smile at a stranger. Flirt. Laugh at a joke. Why not?

Your children are watching you … and want to be like you! A friend told me this one day and I thought; "Help!" To me this felt stressful as if I needed to be a good example to my kids at all times. This was during my burnout and of course, I told myself that I was no good at anything, I thought I was a shouty mother, too perfectionistic and often grumpy. I certainly didn't want my kids to be like that!

My youngest daughter often did not want to give me a kiss in the morning until I had brushed my teeth or had a shower. The words, 'you are stinky mama' came out and she made faces at me. At the time I found it really upsetting and patiently explained to her that you can love and be kind to people whatever they look or smell like. But I also realised later, that it was a phase she went through growing up.

My youngest daughter told me the other day. 'Mama, I think you look pretty. You look pretty with your pyjamas on and no make up, but you look prettier wearing a dress.' Children love it when their parents feel and look good too. That is when their inner beauty can come out too. Children naturally open up when you are smiling and happy. They don't like it when you are sad or grumpy.

Children are amazing levellers. They bring things in life into perspective. They love you for who you are.

When things get tough and there are arguments, I can sometimes criticise myself for not being a good parent. Kids get angry and play up exactly as we do, but they are not as critical on themselves as we are. Children are also brutally honest. When my daughter tells me 'you look pretty, Mama' I know she means it. When she says 'you have smelly breath' I know she means it too!

Children tell you how it is and see past all the small things we criticise ourselves about. We can learn a lot from our children. All they want to do is 'be loved' and spend time with you. And it is beautiful when you see them blossom because of the love and quality time you give them. My kids are so special to me. I am trying to teach them about the world, but in fact they have taught me so much already. They have shown me how to accept myself as I am and not be too critical on myself.

There you go ladies; let go of criticism and accept yourself as you are.

Case Study: Elisa, 38

Elisa had twin boys, but she struggled to be with them at home because she found them so full on. She started to doubt her ability to be a mother and wished she could go back to work. However, once she went back to work, she missed her twin boys. Elisa realised that the reason she struggled with her kids was because she could not take part in the rough and tumble that their dad played with them. Elisa felt inadequate and that she did not have a fun time with her boys. After hearing about my funny face bananas, Elisa decided to try funny faces with her boys' food. She was creative and started to design food on the boy's plate in a face shape. And guess what? Her boys loved it and it was their fun moment together. Success; everybody was happy.

Nerdy Girl

Some days things may not flow in the way you want them to and that is totally okay! For example, when I was all dressed up and on my way to work with dried milk in my hair and I didn't realise it until I arrived at work and went to the toilet. Ahhh…the embarrassment because I looked like the character Mary in the film, *There is Something About Mary!*

The most amusing situation I remember was the one I call 'the skirt incident'. I had bought a black leather pencil skirt and wore it to work when I joined my boss for a meeting one morning.

When I got up to close the door the skirt ripped at the back! I was exposing my whole bum to everyone in the meeting room. Being me, I simply said, 'My skirt has ripped!' and my boss being him – he had a crazy sense of humour – said, 'It wasn't me!' After that, I turned around and walked out of the room like a crab... so no one could see my behind... and dashed to the toilet. I could not fix the skirt, but actually I managed to roll it up so it became a mini skirt, which for some reason seemed to hold it together and hide my bum! I managed to survive the day with the skirt rolled up. Hooray! However, I did have a chuckle later with my colleagues...

Insights

I truly believe positive affirmations help. In fact, they can transform your life. Every morning when I wake up I meditate and repeat positive affirmations; often in the shower! And it gets me in a great mood! It is a perfect way to learn to love yourself better.

For example, when I wake up in the morning, I use the positive affirmation below.

"I love myself and I no longer compare myself with other people."

There is a wonderful book written by Hal Elrod, *The Morning Miracle*. Hal believes that if you get up thirty to sixty minutes earlier in the day and use that time for prayer, meditation, positive affirmations, visualisations and exercise, it will transform your life. Now, this can seem like quite a lot of time, but I really believe it helps. In my case, I use positive affirmations and visualisations because I don't always have time for more than that first thing in the morning.

Practical Tips

1. Affirmations

- Write down a positive affirmation. It can be something you want to happen this year or something you want to change. For example, I attract peace and abundance into my life.
- Keep the affirmation next to your bed.
- Repeat it every day when you wake up; it can become your daily mantra.

2. Praise yourself

- Look at yourself in the mirror every morning and tell yourself you are beautiful.
- Say it out loud.
- Smile when you say it.

3. Take action

- Try out a new lip gloss or lipstick.
- If you are not into make up, think about something else like nice lingerie or new clothes that will make you feel beautiful.

CHAPTER 6

Fire The Good Girl

In this chapter we will explore people pleasing and how to stop being a people pleaser by saying 'no'. We will investigate perfectionism and I will share my experiences about 'expressing myself'. Finally, we will look at how to take charge and be a Queen.

Stop People Pleasing

Do you know that feeling when you want to do the right thing by everybody? You are constantly trying to people please – to do what is expected of you by other people – without really knowing what that is. But you guess, anyway! You are trying to keep everybody happy. This can be to your own detriment because it is actually impossible to please everybody all the time. It is a recipe for disaster. For example, we don't like to cancel when we have set an arrangement with someone because we fear we may be letting them down. Or worse than that they may be angry. Or you know you will feel guilty so rather than live with that guilt you decide to say 'no' to yourself by saying 'yes' to someone else. What if you accept that you can't please everyone all the time, but you can learn instead to be happy yourself and let go of this attitude?

You know that feeling when you don't really want to help other people out, but because you would rather not feel guilty you say 'yes'. Think about this highly relevant and inspirational quote.

"Saying yes to someone else is saying no to yourself".

Paolo Coelho, novelist, writer and lyricist.

I am not saying don't help other people, but I am saying take care of your own needs first. Whatever they may be. You can learn to say 'no' gracefully by thanking the person, but stating that on this occasion it doesn't work for you. And be helpful, by suggesting someone else who can help them or sending them a link to help them sort out their problem.

In Harriet Braiken's book *The Disease to Please: Curing the People Pleasing Syndrome*, she mentions that 'niceness is the psychological armour of the people pleaser'. What it means is that people pleasers like to be nice – they are nice. People pleasers say 'yes' when often they really want to say 'no'.

Harriet's book can help you understand how to live a balanced life and how important it is to put yourself first and not say 'yes' all the time. Harriet explores whether it is selfish to take care of yourself. People pleasers tend to take care of other people's needs first. But actually by not taking care of your own needs, in a roundabout way, you are endangering the people you love. Think about it. You keep doing what you think will please other people, but actually you don't listen to your own inner voice. Eventually, this behaviour will run you down and you can feel unwell. Harriet mentions that when you constantly stress and exhaust yourself by caring for other people at your own expense, you are courting illness, depression and stress. Despite your good intentions, those people who depend on you will suffer as well.

There it is, ladies. Put yourself first and stop people pleasing!

I am no longer a people pleaser these days. I follow my own path and try to let other people down gently if it is not the right time or activity for me. It is not easy though! I find there are moments when I still say 'yes' without thinking and then feel uncomfortable pulling out of a particular event or helping another person. It takes practice!

Say No to Social Stuff

Ladies; stop overcommitting! It is critical to prioritise what is really important to you as an individual and to stop overcommitting. In the Art of Self Care by Cheryl Richardson, she talks about an absolute 'no' list. This is a list that you write for yourself to help you prioritise what is really important and what you don't want to do anymore.

For example, when I did this for myself I wrote the following list.

- I no longer push myself when I am feeling tired and I take time to rest.
- I no longer go to two social events at the weekend; I choose only one and the other day I spend with my family.
- I no longer compare myself to other people.
- I no longer get involved in my children's arguments and I let them sort it themselves. Okay, I will be honest. This one is still a work in progress!
- I no longer feel guilty I can't do everything I want to do.
- I no longer eat a lot of red meat.

Cara's Three Question Exercise

- *Do you know how to say 'no'?*
- *What does saying 'no' mean for you?*
- *Can you think of three things you can say 'no' to and write them down now?*

Having young children, a job and a busy social life can contribute to feeling really tired. Sometimes it is just lovely to be at home with your family and schedule in some 'down time'. Now I hear you. Being at home with a family is not always relaxing. Let's face it. There is mess, countless chores to do and the next meal to think about. But if you can find a small amount of time to enjoy your kids and play with them or simply all 'be' at home, it will give you some breathing space. When I am at home with my husband and kids I find I can easily get into 'doing' mode. Let's put another wash on, sort out the kid's clothes, get the dinner ready, tidy up. There is always something to do. But then I remind myself to focus on 'being' and to take a breather. That is why it is important to consciously say 'now I am going to sit in the garden with a cup of tea' or 'I am going to watch a long movie with my kids' or 'I am going to meditate for 30 minutes'. We live in a world where we all push ourselves to keep 'doing' when actually it is good to relax and simply 'be'.

We all have our own ways of relaxing and 'being'. What are yours?

Trying To Be Perfect

Continually trying to be perfect was definitely a contributing factor to my burnout. For example, when sleep became disrupted I could not accept the fact that I did not sleep the 'recommended' eight hours a night. I thought I would not be able to get through the day. This of course, was not true, but I only came to realise that later on. Perfectionism can be hard work.

Perfectionism is also about trying too hard to please other people. This has certainly been the case for me. Sometimes, I have wanted something to happen and worked very hard towards that outcome. But, I often became frustrated when it didn't happen. Until I discovered that when I let go of the need to have a certain result, miracles happen and things turn out exactly as I had hoped!

Perfectionists tend to spend a lot of time worrying about 'the little things'. A helpful strategy can be to look at the big picture.

Perfectionists find it very hard to accept when things don't go their way. In my case, I have learned to accept things and let them go. My journey of recovery, after my burnout, taught me that actually most things in life can be a bit messy and not everything has to be perfect.

Case Study: Amy, 44

Amy wanted her house to look perfect all the time. She struggled with the mess her kids made and she kept feeling stressed about it. She was tidying up all the time. Eventually, Amy decided that she would have one day a week to tidy up when her kids were at school and nursery. This gave her more time for herself and reduced her stress levels. Now, this nominated day is her 'sacred' cleaning and tidy up day. When she has finished, she celebrates with a cup of tea and a treat. Mission accomplished.

Nerdy Girl

A funny story that actually happened to me demonstrates how it's okay not to be perfect every day.

The British comedian Miranda Hart presents a great sketch on revolving doors, which I decided it might be fun to copy, after a particularly tough day at the office and a broken night's sleep the night before. You know the one, where somebody gets into the compartment for only one person? But then somebody else jumps in with you and you are stuck and squished! I decided to try that with my office revolving doors and jumped into a single compartment with a stranger. The poor guy had such a fright! I quickly apologised of course and told him that I thought 'we would both fit' to which he smiled and walked towards the lifts. I was laughing all the way to the underground station and it really cheered up my day! When I told my husband that evening he told me I was mad!

Express Yourself in the Right Way

If you don't like something or if you don't want to do something then it is much healthier and better for everyone if you say it out loud in your own words. If it is hard for you to say and you are worried about 'blurting it out' then practice it by writing it down first. I have often blurted things out in the past without thinking how best to word them. These days I take a step back and review what I really want to say. Writing it down before you speak to the other person helps. You can give people feedback in a positive, careful way. Although of course, not everyone will always agree with what you say or believe you have communicated it well! Now, I am not talking about doing this on social media but actually speaking to people and communicating. This can be your partner, your children – gently – and your family, friends and your co-workers. Hateful messages on social media do not work. I believe that it helps to communicate better and tell people how you are feeling. But do it in the right way – think about it – and express it carefully. Speak to them in person.

Let's be honest, I am only human so sometimes that does not work. There have been plenty of times when all I have wanted to do was tell a loved one I was feeling hurt or upset about something but did not word it in a way that they understood. They took it as criticism, or misunderstood my communication as anger or jealousy. This got their backs up and ended in a full-blown argument, which was not what I intended at all. Lessons learned ladies!

Being outspoken and assertive and telling people what you want and don't want is a sure way to fire the 'Good Girl'. You can take hold of the reigns and be successful by treating yourself with greater love. This in turn will make you stronger.

How to Take Charge; You Are the Queen

How do you take charge? Those limiting beliefs can come back with niggly questions like: What if I don't have enough confidence? What if I don't feel it?

We all have limiting beliefs. It is very easy to believe those negative inner questions and to convince yourself that you can't change. Or if you say "no" to people you won't be able to live with yourself. And that is okay. This takes practice. You can start today!

Don't over-commit. Write down your list of priorities. And keep at it. It takes practice to stop people pleasing and to say 'no'. But you can do it. Keep thinking of the long-term benefits. For example, you will have more time for yourself and less stress.

Women have been raised to be caregivers and to nurture, which is often why it is so hard for us to say 'no'. Your inner voice will say 'but I do really want to help'.

How about this? The next time you are asked to do something – take a deep breath first – and seriously think if you can spare the time and energy. Will you feel more upset at yourself for doing it or more upset at yourself for NOT doing it? Which option is better for you?

Never rely solely on other people for praise. Write down three things you did well each day and keep reminding yourself you can do it! Be proud of yourself!

Insights

It has taken me a long time to learn to say 'no' and put myself first. But wow, has it been worth it. I live a much more balanced and peaceful life. Now, I say 'yes' to the things that are really important to me and to us as a family.

Fire The Good Girl

Practical Tips

1. Prioritise

- Write down your list of priorities and start saying 'no'. Prioritise yourself!

2. Communicate clearly

- Talk to other people when you are not happy about something; never suffer in silence.

3. Let go

- Stop trying to be perfect; let it go.
- Never rely on other people for praise.

CHAPTER 7

Structure for Wellbeing

In this chapter we will investigate adrenal fatigue, I will share my own experiences and we will focus on mindful cooking and eating. Finally, we will explore how to put good energy into your food.

Set Your Intentions

It is important to set your intentions in terms of physical wellbeing. Are you eating well and nourishing your body or simply grabbing whatever you can? Are you cooking well for the kids but not yourself? Put nourishing and healthy foods in your body, although I know this is sometimes easier said than done when you are busy.

Diet

For years I watched my weight and tried to be healthy. Most of the time my priority was staying slim and fit. Since my early forties, I have started to experience first-hand the benefits of eating right for wellbeing. I noted that after drinking a strong cup of coffee I sweated more and felt anxious. I never used to experience this before. "How weird", I thought.

I went to see a naturopath who introduced me to food supplements such as magnesium, which is known as nature's tranquiliser and a mineral, which many people are deficient in. Talk to your healthcare provider or health food specialist before you buy any supplements. Get the right advice tailored to your needs. My naturopath also recommended B vitamins because they can help in times of stress. She also suggested I take a good multivitamin and vitamins C and D in the winter.

But I felt something was not quite right so I went to see a nutritionist. She suggested I get my adrenal glands tested. She suspected that following my burnout my adrenal glands where out of whack and therefore my hormones. This would explain the sweating and anxiety after drinking a cup of coffee. Coffee can put stress on the body and can cause cortisol to rise. Your body detects this as a 'fight or flight' mode and reacts.

It turned out that my adrenal glands were not balanced. I was shocked. I had been eating healthily and looking after myself so how could this be possible? Apparently, sometimes it can take the body years to recover from burnout. My nutritionist suggested I cut out gluten and milk, had less coffee and alcohol. After only 10 days of cutting out cow's milk and only drinking almond or coconut milk, I started to feel better and I had much more energy.

What are Adrenals?

The adrenal glands are situated on top of the kidneys. The human body has two adrenal glands that release chemicals called hormones into the bloodstream. These hormones affect many parts of the human body, including: controlling energy production; fluid balance; fat storage; sex hormone production and stress response.

In Susan Scott's book on burnout, she states that 'the adrenals have a normal daily rhythm of manufacturing and releasing cortisol.

When you first wake up in the morning, you release a surge of cortisol into the bloodstream. Cortisol is a stimulating hormone, which helps you to get up and get going. You continue to naturally release cortisol for the rest of the day, but in smaller amounts. Eventually, at the end of the day, levels will be low enough for you to go back to sleep. This is normal cortisol rhythm. When you have a stressful day, instead of releasing diminishing amounts of cortisol, your adrenals react by ensuring that the amount of cortisol remains elevated. This helps you to cope, but you are in 'fight or flight' mode. When you continue without giving yourself time to switch off and recover, your adrenals and the receptors around the body that receive the cortisol hormone, will be overworked, exhausted and unable to function sufficiently. When this happens you can no longer produce enough cortisol to meet your demands and your cortisol levels remain low all day'.

This can eventually lead to adrenal fatigue.

The body can perceive all kinds of different stress in the same way; this can be fear, worry, pain, inflammation, infection or lack of sleep. The body only has one way to respond and this is through the adrenal hormones and the stress response. The great news is we can do something about it by relieving stress and improving our nutrition and taking more exercise. Seeing a nutritionist and getting the right advice on nutrition helped me balance my hormones and reduce the amount of stress I felt on a day-to-day basis?

Nicki Williams at *Happy Hormones for Life* offers great tailored programmes that look at every aspect of your life and how to balance hormones. She is an award-winning nutritionist and hormone expert. Her vision is that every woman in their 40s and

50s can feel better than they did in their 30s. She offers women, who are needlessly suffering, the missing support they need to naturally rebalance their hormones and return to their best health, through guided support, nutrition and online programmes. She has also recently published her first book on the subject, which is called *It's Not You, It's Your Hormones; The essential guide for women over 40 to fight fat, fatigue and hormone havoc.*

Nerdy Girl

A few years ago a friend convinced me to go on a detox retreat in Thailand. I thought it was a wonderful idea and was very excited about detoxing my body and losing weight. I was not aware of how amazing I would feel after not eating anything – really we only drank coconut water and diluted melon juice – for a whole week!

However, my husband could not understand why I would fly all the way to Thailand and not eat any of the delicious Thai food. He was convinced I was secretly barbequing geckos in my room every night! I remember feeling so hungry I actually considered eating any bugs or geckos running about!

I will never go for a whole week without eating again. The experience taught me a wonderful lesson about how much junk we put into our bodies. Once rid of that junk, my body was cleansed and detoxed and it was very grateful and rewarded me with amazing energy and love. I felt absolutely fabulous!

I also remember the feeling of reintroducing dairy, alcohol and sugar again. I added them back into my diet slowly as I was advised to do. But after a dinner out with my boyfriend one night – ironically we went to a Thai restaurant because I was craving the food – I felt sick. I drank one glass of wine, had a main meal and desert, but it was enough to send my poor body into shock! I felt sick that night and it continued all of the next day. It was quite bizarre.

Interestingly, I had felt unwell for a day or two into the detox. This is apparently normal, especially if you are used to drinking caffeine daily and you get the caffeine withdrawal headache. The detox also presented me with weird dreams, so vivid and scary. It also brought on my monthly cycle about two weeks earlier than normal. But once I got through the first few days, I felt better and had more energy than I had experienced for year-. It was no wonder that going back to my "normal" diet made me feel strange.

Chocolate and Sweeties

Yes ladies, I admit it; I have been a chocoholic all my life. It started when I was a little girl and my parents took us to the local sweet shop on Saturdays. I bought a small bag of chocolate and sweeties with my pocket money! This was our weekly treat.

I just love chocolate! Especially at Easter, when the little chocolate eggs are in abundance. "Ah just one more won't hurt", I tell myself. Until I get to the end of the day and wonder why I am not feeling hungry...too many chocolate eggs!

Before I had kids I used to visit the local corner shop with my friend because I was craving chocolate raisins. The owner, who I might add, was a brilliant salesman, didn't have any chocolate raisins, but he recommended I bought chocolate and raisins and smashed them together. 'It will make you chocolate raisins,' he said. I loved his selling tactic and it worked!

These days I am a dark chocolate convert. I actually eat a teeny weeny bit every day. Yes every day! Years ago I would have beaten myself up for that, but now I enjoy it and allow myself this delicious treat. One small square of chocolate a day. But does it keep the doctor away?

There have been significant studies in the last few years about chocolate. Countless media reports have been published, but often the findings are exaggerated or they can leave out important details.

However, it is interesting to note that the European Food Safety Authority (EFSA) has actually only approved one study in 2012, which states: 'that Cocoa Flavanols help maintain the elasticity of blood vessels, which contributes to normal blood flow'. And to obtain the effect, 200 mg of Cocoa Flavanols should be consumed daily. That could be 10 grams of high Flavanol dark chocolate or 2.5 gram of high Flavanol Cocoa powder. Unfortunately, there are only a few specialist producers who have been able to produce chocolate with high Flavanol and these are usually not for sale in high street shops.

So, is dark chocolate healthy?

Well, it is also important to know that chocolate still has fat and sugar in it so can be eaten as a treat in very small quantities. Eating too much of the stuff is not good for you! While it is difficult to be totally sure about the health effects, it seems probably that there are health benefits to our heart's health as per the EFSA study.

Remember to buy a good quality dark chocolate. Over the years my tastes have changed and I am now a huge dark chocolate fan. It stops me from eating too much of it too because after the experience of eating a whole bar of 70% dark chocolate in one go I was jumping off the walls!

Mindful Cooking and Eating

The most important thing about eating healthily is to set your intentions. You can change your state of mind by committing to put good loving energy into your food. Never grab and eat mindlessly.

When I started weaning my first baby, it seemed like a lot of hard work – blending sweet potato and different vegetables and fruits to see if she liked them. But this was nothing compared to the double whammy of adult meals, pre-schooler meals and toddler meals, all at the same time. It became really confusing and stressful for me. I was cooking something for my husband and myself, then another meal for my three year old and something different for my baby. I wanted to do it all 'right' and make sure they got all the right foods and nutrients.

These days, there is so much pressure on parents to feed their children healthy nutritious meals. It is definitely a positive thing, but it can be stressful too.

I have found that getting organised really helps. Batch cooking is my solution! Whenever you are cooking a meal for the family – cook a larger portion and freeze the leftovers. Then you always have something ready when the family are hungry and you don't feel like cooking from scratch. You can also freeze baby purees and baby foods.

Case Study: Frankie, 29

Frankie worked full time, but had a nanny to look after her baby. She made sure there was enough food for the nanny and her baby in the fridge, but often she bought a takeaway for herself and her husband. She started putting on weight and couldn't work out why. Frankie realized that she was not focusing on herself and was so tired at the end of the day that she didn't feel like cooking. She took my advice and started to cook larger quantities and freeze them for future meals. It improved things drastically for Frankie as she is now eating healthy home cooked meals that only take five minutes to warm up. When she started to concentrate on eating more healthily and cooking at home, she lost weight and felt much better in herself.

Cara's Three Question Exercise

- *Is healthy food important to you?*
- *What do you want to put into your meals?*
- *Do you want to achieve: more energy; lose weight; or balance your hormones?*

How to Put Good Energy into Your Food

I have often found myself annoyed when cooking for my children. I would be rushing and trying to do several things at the same time. But now I take time to breathe and be mindful when I cook. You can listen to music and simply focus on positive thoughts. I hear you though. You are thinking; 'How is it possible to have positive thoughts when the kids are going mental around me?' Let's face it. It may not always be possible, but when you set your positive intentions you are already half way there. Before you start to cook, think positive thoughts, take a deep breath and notice and enjoy the smells and flavours.

Did you know that there are some plants that help clean the air in your house? I have these wonderful plants called Peace Lilies; their Latin name is Spathiphyllum. They are a beautiful dark green colour with white flowers that have been proven to cleanse the air inside houses. They also create a peaceful feeling. I also love fresh flowers. I always try to have some freshly cut flowers on our kitchen table. Flowers can bring positive vibes to your house.

Insights

I was sceptical about how nutrition and mindful cooking can help. But ladies, it really does. Putting nutritious foods and beverages in your body can give you so much more energy and make you feel amazing. And it totally helps you be organised and make sure you never grab food.

Practical Tips

1. Be mindful about what food you buy, how you cook and eat

- Go organic when you can.
- Set your intentions to cook with a positive attitude; even when the kids are driving you nuts!

2. Get organised, plan an hour to batch cook and freeze meals!

- Plan your meals in advance and buy in bulk.

3. Be good to your hormones

- Having good nutrition and taking supplements can help balance your hormones, but it is important to get the right advice for your body and your specific needs.

CHAPTER 8

Be Kind

In this chapter we will explore the importance of being kind to yourself and to other people. I will share my own experiences and we will look at how you can learn to love and accept yourself. Finally, we will explore how to be grateful to yourself.

Be Kind to Yourself and Other People

What does being kind actually mean? It can have several meanings. Being kind to yourself means you take care of yourself; you respect yourself and you forgive yourself. It can mean you are more gentle with yourself and are able to soothe yourself. There are so many ways to be kind to yourself. But what is clear is that by being kind to yourself you will feel better about yourself and this will help you take better care of other people too.

Accept Yourself

A good way to start being kind to yourself is by accepting yourself completely. It is easy to accept the part of you that is happy, joyful, in love or funny or strong. But what about other characteristics like anger, envy or jealousy? Most people find it much harder to accept these emotions and sometimes push them away.

We all have these feelings, but most of us find them difficult to accept or we beat ourselves up about feeling what we call 'negative emotions'. Everyone has a darker side and if you embrace that side of you and treat it with love, this will help you accept yourself. We all have good sides and not so good sides. But when you can learn to accept your dark side, as well as the radiant, you can love your whole self.

Accepting yourself also means accepting we can't do it all sometimes. Be realistic with yourself and accept the areas that you may not be handling as well. Are you in a successful career, but feel you are stuck as a mum or are you a great mum, but have had to take a step back in your career? How is your weight? How is your self-worth?

Practice self-acceptance and self-compassion. You can take charge and accept yourself for who you are. You can define your own worth. This does not have to be decided by other people. You can practice this self-compassion meditation, which only takes a few minutes and when practised regularly, can really change your mindset.

Sit down in a comfortable place. Close your eyes and take a deep breath. Repeat these phrases.

- I love myself deeply.
- I accept myself as I am.
- I am peaceful and happy.

When you can change your mindset, it is hugely powerful. You will feel more powerful, simply because you love yourself. Your success is in looking after yourself and treating yourself with great love.

Cara's Three Question Exercise

- *Can you accept yourself as you are?*
- *Do you know how to soothe yourself?*
- *In what way are you kind to yourself?*

Be Positive!

Be kind to yourself. Avoid saying negative things about yourself and other people. It is important to choose to be around positive people and stay positive about yourself as well. I know this is tough. But it is scientifically proven that it is possible to reduce worry by replacing negative thoughts with positive ones. Notice when you are feeling negative or having negative thoughts and replace them with positive ones.

Remember to calm and turn off that little voice in your head, which tells you off and berates you. The voice who says; "I should have". Don't tune into that voice; use positive affirmations instead. After a while, your brain will start to listen to them more clearly and let the voice go. For example when your inner critic is telling you should have answered and email in a different way; or you should have stayed at work longer because your colleague did; or you should not have shouted at your child. Turn it around and say: I answered the email in the best way at the time and it was a great response; or I needed to leave work for some 'me time'; or when I raised my voice to my child it became clear that mummy was teaching her something important.

There are several other definitions of 'kind' in the dictionaries. However, the ones that jumped out at me were 'generous, helpful and thinking about other people's feelings' and 'not causing harm or damage'. Everyone has a different understanding of 'being kind'. What is yours?

When I worked in central London, I often walked from Waterloo Station across the river, past Trafalgar Square and to my office. There was an area next to the square where I was always shocked and upset to see lots of homeless people on the street. I was so upset by it that one day I was stopped by a charity worker on the street and I decided to support his charity. He asked me to support 'houses for the homeless'. I signed up straight away. Here I was – living a comfortable life with a roof over my head – while thousands of other people are without a warm home. I started giving away to the homeless people outside the train station any free food samples I had received.

I have been very grateful to strangers helping me in the past. For example, the men and women who have helped me during pregnancy or who helped me carry a pushchair up the stairs in a metro station, which I now always do for women if I can manage to carry the buggy. A smile; a friendly look; asking if you are okay? These little acts of kindness mean so much to people.

We can all be stuck in our own little world on the daily commute to work. Nobody enjoys it. But you can look up and around you. Make eye contact with people. Smile.

Two days before my second child was due to be born, I was very uncomfortable. It was a very hot summer and our flat was boiling. I could not cool down. I walked from the supermarket where there was air-conditioning to the cinema and back. But on that specific day I could not even make it back home. I felt so faint that when I walked past my local coffee shop – which was closed – I saw the owner inside and knocked on the door. He took me in and gave me an iced drink. He turned on the air-conditioning and helped me cool down. I sat there for a long time. I was so grateful to that wonderful man.

Many of us are too busy with our mobile phones and our public image to notice things these days. People spend so much time on their phones and less time having contact with real people. And it doesn't make us any happier. People are searching for something fulfilling. Kindness unlocks something deep. When we are kind to someone it doesn't only help that person, but it is scientifically proven to improve our own physical and mental health. Look around. Maybe that old lady would benefit from a chat? Or the pregnant lady is suffering. Help that person. We all need it.

Case Study: Fran, 47

Fran narrowly avoided burnout when she was the CEO of a local charity in her first management role. When her daughter was one year old, she and her husband took in a vulnerable young woman to live with them because she had Post Traumatic Stress Disorder and needed support. It was a stressful time for Fran with lots of high-level responsibility coming from all angles. Fran had two mini strokes and realised she had to take better care of herself. She was put on Beta Blockers in the first instance. But then, she started meditating, jogging and learning about self-compassion. Fran also learned to retrain her inner voice and be more friendly and forgiving with herself. She now takes good care of herself, which in turn means she can help her family and other people better.

How to be Kind to Other People

The more you practice kindness to other people, the happier you will be.

"This is my simple religion. There is no need for temples, no need for complicated philosophy. Our own brain, our own heart is our temple. The philosophy is kindness."

18th Dalai Lama

I have always enjoyed sending cards and small gifts to friends and family. Once I even sent a friend a small chocolate bar in the post – no note needed! Write thank you notes; send cards and letters, containing small gifts. Send them to family and friends – give it a try – you will feel good about it.

Give compliments. When you think that someone looks nice – even if they are a complete stranger – tell them. It will cheer them up and it will cheer you up too. For example, a nice dress, their hair, shoes or their laugh. Everyone likes to be complimented. It will help them shine and have a great day and it will help you too.

The Power of Healing

Following my burnout, there continued to be a lot I needed to process. I was holding on to anger, mainly with myself for letting the burnout happen. I was not able to let go and was holding on to emotional pain.

Being the oldest child in my family, I always felt responsible for everyone and felt that I needed to hold it all together. After recovering from burnout, I noticed how I was still angry with myself and frustrated in my job. I sought the help of a Transformational Coach. I was not happy where I was in my work and I needed to release these 'negative emotions' so I could move on to the next chapter of my life, which was going to be my coaching, hosting workshops and writing this book, to help other people.

I met a wonderful Transformational Coach called, Gosia Gorna and wow, did she transform things for me! Gosia helped me deal with my fears and to heal myself using a powerful tool she calls *The Expansion Game*. Gosia transformed my life in so many ways; she helped me get to where I am now and to connect with many amazing women. Miracles started to happen when I met Gosia.

I truly believe that healing yourself is about being kind to yourself and this helps you to become more powerful and have an amazing impact on other people. Being softer and kinder with yourself can actually help you to be more powerful. Wow! We don't need to be superwomen; we can be powerful by looking after ourselves and being kind to ourselves.

A few months after first consulting Gosia, I went to see a Reiki Healer. I had no idea what Reiki was about. But wow, that stuff is powerful! I am someone who holds onto a lot of personal baggage. It took a long time for my body to relax during the first session. Once I did, it felt amazing. I felt emotions come up and halfway through the treatment I started to cry. Of course, Nerdy Girl apologised profusely for crying...

I highly recommend Reiki. It is so great and actually more emotions came out as the days went on.

Healing yourself is the key to being able to move on in your life.

Nerdy Girl

I started being kinder to myself and having regular relaxing baths, using lovely lavender, other essential oils and Epsom salts; although not all at the same time! It was my special time to relax and be alone. My children have their bath toys next to the bath. One night by a bizarre twist of fate, I found myself having a bath with the whole Simpson family. First, Homer Simpson fell in with a big splash! Next, I was joined by Bart Simpson, Marge Simpson, Lisa Simpson and little baby Simpson. Before I knew it, I had the entire plastic cartoon Simpson family, from the infamous television series, in my bath! It gave me a big shock. The toy basket next to the bath had broken and the toys were falling out into the bath… I shrieked out loud and when my husband came upstairs to see what was going on he started laughing.

'I can't believe you are playing with the children's toys,' was his response with a chuckle. It was an interesting situation, but such fun!

How to be Grateful for Yourself

Having a bath is a lovely way of looking after yourself. It is loving and kind. At the end of the day, before bed I get out my journal and write down three things I am grateful for that happened during the day. I often write how grateful I am for myself and the things I am proud of.

We often find it hard to be grateful for ourselves. It can seem a bit 'stuck up' or over the top. And I was one of these people. I was far too hard on myself. Now, I write how grateful I am for myself 'just the way I am' – like the Bridget Jones movie. Try it, ladies – write down how grateful you are for yourself – exactly as you are, right now.

Or I am grateful for…looking after myself today.

Thank yourself with small rewards and treats such as your favourite beverage, a book, a magazine, a bath; whatever takes your fancy!

Many of us find it easier to be grateful for other people, but not as easy to be grateful for ourselves. Especially if you are hard on yourself or a perfectionist. But with small steps and self-care, you can learn to love and be grateful for yourself. You can show gratitude for yourself by being kind to yourself.

Insights

It is so important to be kind to yourself and other people. Accept yourself and be grateful for yourself. If it starts with you, then this can spread and we can all learn to be kinder and nicer to each other. Kindness is contagious. This world can be really harsh; bring some kindness into it. That may have a ripple effect on others too.

It is important to be realistic and know that you can't do it all and it is okay to drop the ball sometimes.

Practical Tips

1. Accept yourself as you are

- Yes ladies, that also means accepting the traits you don't like. You are wonderful exactly the way you are right now!
- Be realistic, you can't do it all and that is okay!

2. Do nice things for yourself and other people

- Buy someone a coffee, help a friend, or smile at a stranger.
- Give compliments.

3. Practice self-compassion.

- Be grateful
- Write down three things every night you are grateful for; one of them has to include you!

CHAPTER 9

Connect With Other Women

In this chapter we explore the importance of connecting with other women in the workplace and other mums. I describe my own experiences and finally, we investigate why female friendships are so important. We also look closely at the importance of delegating.

It is so important to connect with other women. There is a wonderful article in the online magazine, *Uplift* that talks about the why it is important for women to have their tribe. In the olden days women connected much more. They shared the care of their children, cooked together and collected food together. This network comforted women and gave them strength. These days we are more isolated. Families do not always live near to each other. We can miss this wonderful healing, nourishing feeling that comes from being with each other. Because women are carers and nurturers it is very important that we receive, as well as give. But many of us don't receive and we end up only giving. Giving all the time can deplete us and it can lead to burnout. Women know how to heal and look after each other. Women help each other. We share a special bond. We open up to each other more easily. Female friendship is the most wonderful thing. When we have good strong female friendships it can really help us reduce stress or overwhelm.

During the years, I have built up an amazing group of girlfriends. I am so lucky to have them and I am grateful for these dear friends every day. I have good friends close to where I live, but also they are spread out around the world too. It is important to have local friends, but these days it doesn't matter if a friend lives further away. For example, I have amazing friends who live in New Zealand. All we need to do sometimes is have a call by FaceTime, Snap Chat, Skype, Zoom, Hangout or WhatsApp. It doesn't have to be long, but simply to connect and hear each other's voices; hear what is going on for that person at that moment. And we give each other nudges, if we think the other person needs to implement more self-care or take some time out. It is a deep connection. I have some wonderful local friends as well. Friendships can change over the years too. Sometimes, you are closer to one friend at one point in your life than other friends. It can be a gentle, continuing flow.

Many studies across the world show that friendship has a bigger impact on our psychological wellbeing than family relationships. There was a wonderful Ted Talk in December 2015, by Jane Fonda and Lily Tomlin where they talked about the power of female friendships. Jane Fonda mentioned that research has shown how women respond differently to stress. When we experience stress the 'fight or flight' response is triggered and the Cortisol hormone is released. Another hormone called Oxytocin is also released by stress. For many women, this Oxytocin can help women look after their children and get together with other women. So, when we make friends with other women, more Oxytocin is released and this helps us calm down. Jane Fonda also mentioned that for a long time women were not included in stress research because of monthly hormonal fluctuations.

In Jane's talk she mentions that men and women respond to stress in a different ways. Men produce high levels of the hormone Testosterone when they are under stress, which can reduce levels of Oxytocin. Women produce Estrogen and this enhances the effect of Oxytocin and this helps them to seek support from other women. It is proven that support during difficult times can alleviate your mood. In Jane Fonda's and Lily Tomlin's Ted talk, you can see that they have been friends for a long time because make fun of each other. It is a jokey friendship. Jane Fonda also talks about how it is important to have different kind of friends and I agree with her.

There are friends who you can have a coffee with, friends you can do sports with, school friends, study friends, tough time friends, party friends, friends who will make you laugh, friends whose shoulder you can cry on and vice versa.

Support Systems at Work

It is also very important to connect with other women at work. When I went through my burnout, I isolated myself. I did not talk to anyone about what had happened because I felt embarrassed by it. After a while, however, I started opening up and talking to other people at work about it. I built a supportive network of female colleagues around me who I felt I trusted. I shared my story and other people started opening up to me too. I started to help other women at work. Through the grapevine other colleagues contacted me when they heard that I helped people with burnout and overwhelm. What a positive shift!

Many companies today have women's network groups you can join or you can be bold and set up your own. For example, in previous companies where I worked there was often a strong support mechanism between the executive assistants. This group met regularly and helped each other out wherever possible.

Mama's Support

If you are a Mama then I suggest you make Mama friends – these wonderful friends who are also mums – can be your part of your tribe. If you have kids your mum friends simply "get you". We all know what it is like to have young children and we help each other; at school pickups, nursery and play dates. I used to be afraid to ask for help from other mums; I didn't like feeling I owed them something. But now I know we are all there to help each other. So, get your mama posse together! When women get together it can be very powerful. There are a group of wonderful mum friends I meet up with regularly. When we meet it is so good for our souls. It is soul food. We laugh, we chat, we cry, we talk about bad stuff and good stuff. We joke. But we feel connected and support each other and that is a great feeling. Lean on your mama network ladies. They will help you get through the tough times!

Nerdy Girl

I also have a group of wonderful girlfriends I met when I was studying in the Netherlands. We have known each other for more than 25 years and have seen each other through many of life's changes, the good and the bad times. Years ago, I used to send this group and other friends a joke every week. In Dutch, I called it, *minimoppentrommel*. I was convinced that everyone saw the humour and enjoyed the jokes. I must admit they were not always that funny, but I kept sending them out every week. Until one day one of my friends told me she really didn't think they were funny! I was heartbroken! Well not really because I knew they were not great jokes, but it was my way of communicating and keeping in touch in a light way. However, I valued her honesty and now it is something we joke about, together.

The Power of Boundaries

Most of us are doing too much activity these days. The rapid arrival of technology has created additional stress and increased activity in our lives. The rapid speed of life, the media and business; our world has dramatically changed pace. Burnout and stress are reaching epidemic levels and it is time to take action; but in a gentle way! I have found that prioritising and delegating are both very effective ways to start minimising overwhelm and stress.

Start prioritising Write down a list of things in your life that are important to you, right now. Remember to write down what is important, not what is urgent. Keep this list close and look at it every day to remind yourself what is important in your life. Whether that is: your family; friends; health; or anything else. Keep it in mind when things get crazy busy.

Set boundaries for yourself and in your relationships This includes relationships at work and with friends. Set boundaries with yourself too. Keep a promise you make to yourself. For example, when I come home after work I will be with the kids and not check my phone or emails. Keep that list of priorities in mind.

Delegate One way to combat overwhelm is to delegate. I run a session about it in my workshops and I have had many clients come back to me to say how relieved they felt after they were able to delegate some of the tasks on their list.

In an article by *Motherly*, a modern lifestyle magazine and brand which is redefining motherhood, Lisa Druxman talks about how a Chief Executive Officer delegates. So, that means a Chief of Everything (a mum) can delegate too. But you may wonder who you can delegate to? Or you might be thinking that you don't have the time to teach someone to do what you need to do so you may as well do it yourself. Or perhaps you can't afford to delegate.

The fact of the matter is that it is easier than you think; here is how to do delegate effectively.

- Write a list of items that are causing you stress at the moment.
- Decide which items you can delegate; go on, let it go! Letting go is key if you want to delegate. There must be at least one thing on your list that you can delegate. For example, can you delegate your chores; the cleaning; shopping; or perhaps a few hours of childcare? Can you find someone to help you out once a week?
- Think about who you can delegate to at work. Do you have an assistant? Or a junior you can ask to help you out on a few tasks? Or can you ask one of your peers to help you out? If you are a business owner, then virtual assistance is amazing these days. You can get so much delegated from the comfort of your own home. For example, a virtual PA can help you organise a party, your calendar and meetings, as well as any travel you may have coming up.

Once you have identified what you can let go of and the person who is best suited to help you, then chat to them about it. This is the hardest part for most people because many successful women find it really hard to ask for help. In the past I have found it hard to ask for help because I did not want to appear 'needy'. There was a vulnerability in asking for help that the 'I can do it all woman' in me didn't want to feel.

Asking for help is crucial if you want to avoid burnout. Getting support and taking care of your needs is fundamental and by being more gentle with yourself you can, in return, avoid burnout. So, ladies here you go. It is so important to learn to ask for help. Try it with one small thing and see how it goes. But be very specific in what you ask for. Not 'maybe, I need help with that presentation or I need an hour away from the kids'. For example, when I was creating the new website for Softer Success I asked two people to give me their thoughts about a specific page or colour scheme etc. When you ask someone for help, most of the time they are happy to help you. Be gracious and accepting. Do not beat yourself up or feel guilty that you are not doing it yourself. It is crucial you get that help to have less stress and overwhelm in your life, which will in turn prevent burnout.

Let go; pinpoint who can help you; give clear instructions; and trust they will get the job done. You can oversee and teach them, or perhaps learn from them as you go along.

You can also delegate to your kids. For example, I know mums who get their kids to make their own packed lunches. A few years ago when my kids were very little I met up with a friend for lunch. Her three children were 7, 9 and 11 years old. I was talking to her about making my kid's breakfast and she simply said. 'Oh, my boys get their own breakfast now'. This seemed impossible to me but now my children are older they actually like to prepare their own packed lunches; but let's get real…this doesn't happen every day.

When my kids were little, I had to be very hands-on with them. But as they grow older, I am giving them more freedom and I let them experience more activities by themselves. For example:

I asked my six year old daughter what day it was the next day and when she answered 'Tuesday; it is ballet tomorrow', I could see her mind working...Then, she started to think of getting her ballet things ready for the next day. She was learning to think and plan for herself.

How to Connect Via Groups and Workshops

The world of social media can be quite daunting for many people these days. There are so many groups and places to connect. But the question is, where do you go for support? Of course I want to suggest you come to one of my Softer Success workshops or follow me on social media. I share tips and tricks about how to be more gentle with yourself. In the workshops, we look at ways of relieving stress, overwhelm and changing your mindset to prevent burnout. These are lovely, gentle and relaxing events and we do meditations and visualisations as well.

Workshops and groups are also a great way to connect with women in person and make new friendships. I am a strong advocate of meeting like-minded people.

But if workshops or groups are not for you, then what about joining a gym or a yoga class? They are a great way to meet other people, expand your tribe and make new friends.

Case Study: Natasha, 39

When I first met Natasha, she was already focusing on her personal development following a burnout. But what gave her a huge feeling of support was meeting like-minded women in my workshop. Suddenly, she did not feel so alone and she shared her anxieties with new people, which was a brave thing to do. She was brave and vulnerable at the same time and everyone respected that and liked her for her honesty. She connected with many people in the workshop and afterwards they continued talking and sharing tips and advice. They exchanged telephone numbers and have continued to support each other since the workshop, which has been rewarding for them and for me too!

Cara's Three Question Exercise

- *Are you able to confide and share with other people?*
- *Do you have a group of women you connect and share information about your life with regularly?*
- *Can you help each other out?*

Insights

A community of women is an extremely strong force. Do not underestimate the power that a group of women have together. Connect with other women as much as possible; find your tribe; create your posse. That special group of women who will support you no matter what happens.

Practical Tips

1. Create your tribe

- Find your girl posse, your tribe of women who keep you sane and stay in touch with them regularly.

2. Community connection

- Join workshops and local groups and have more fun too!

3. Ask for help

- Think about who you can ask for help from and then delegate tasks at home and at work, to reduce your action list. This will relieve the pressure to do it all yourself.

Epilogue; Softer Success Redefined

Now that we have been on this journey together, it is time for you to apply what you have learned about a gentler, kinder success in your life; a Softer Success.

We learned about understanding and celebrating the changes that take place when you have children; we looked at prioritising yourself; taking time out and the power of meditation and of gratitude. We also learned how important it is to express your feelings and connect with other women. Now you have learned that success can be defined by taking care of yourself better, it is time to take the actions to embed this into your life, using all the tips and tricks I have provided. After years of pushing myself to keep going and do more and more all the time and thinking that by trying to be Super Woman I would achieve what I wanted, I have now found a more gentle, softer way of being. By being gentle with myself I have achieved a Softer Success, which for me means living a healthy, balanced, peaceful and happy life.

I have learned to be gentle with myself by learning to be more self-aware. There are times when I have started to feel tightness in my shoulders or tiredness in my body. But I know these signals now and I listen to them. I give myself permission to take a break from what I am doing and I practice yoga or meditation instead. The key to achieving Softer Success every day is giving yourself permission to be gentle with yourself; to take that break; to meditate; to turn off your inner critic and to simply be you.

In this book, I have redefined success as a Softer Success and, as a result, my own life has become more gentle too. Now, it is your turn. Having read my book, can you redefine your own success? For example, by:

- not squeezing too much activity into your days;
- taking time to be;
- taking time out for self-care;
- practising self-love and self-acceptance;
- letting go and
- slowing down.

I truly believe when we can learn to be more gentle with ourselves, we can, in turn, prevent stress and burnout. If we as a generation can do this, then the next generation will thank us for leading the way and they can follow suit. It doesn't mean we are weak and can't achieve things. On the contrary, it means we are taking control of self-care and self-love. We can redefine success by slowing down and taking time to be. Slowly; softly; gently.

This is how we can become more powerful than ever before.

Give yourself permission for a Softer Success.

I wish you the best; with love for a Softer Success

Cara de Lange

Contact Cara

Website: www.softersuccess.com

Facebook: Softer Success

Instagram: @softersuccess

LinkedIn: https://www.linkedin.com/in/ caradelange/

Email: cara@softersuccess.com

Chapter References

Introduction

- *A Kinder Gentler Philosophy of Success*;
  Alain de Botton, Ted Talk, 28 July 2009

Chapter 1

- Professor John Studd, Consultant gynaecologist, www.studd.co.uk

- *Pregnancy Changes Brain Structure*,
  Elseline Hoekzema, Nature Neuroscience, 19th December 2016

Chapter 2

- Nicola Bird; *A little piece of mind*
  http://www.alittlepeaceofmind.co.uk

- NUK blog; *Be guilt free*; 1 February 2016

- World Health Organisation, World Health Report: *Mental Disorders affect one in four people*

- World Health Organisation, *Comprehensive Mental Health Action Plan 2013-2020*

- World Health Organisation, *The World Health Organisation's Global Plan of Action on Worker's Health 2008-2017*

- *Five Balls of Life* Speech by former Coca Cola CEO, Brian Dyson

Chapter 3

- *The Young Professionals guide on how to prevent burnout*, Susan Scott,
  Filament Publishing, 2017

- Roger Ekirch, *Day's Close: Night in Times Past*, October 2006

- Dr Nerina Ramlakhan, www.drnerina.com

- The Next Web on 7th August 2017, www.thenextweb.com

- *Is social media bad for you?*, BBC, 5th January, 2018, http://www.bbc.com/future/story/20180104-is-social-media-bad-for-you-the-evidence-and-the-unknowns

Chapter 4

- www.calm.com, daily calm meditation, March 2018

- www.bakker.com, gardening poll 2015

Chapter 5

- *When I Loved Myself Enough*, Karen McMillen, Board book, 2001

- *Mama Gena's School of Womanly Arts*, Simon & Schuster, 2003

- Amy Cuddy Ted Talk, October 2012, https://www.ted.com/talks/amy_cuddy_your_body_language_shapes_who_you_are

- *The Morning Miracle: The 6 Habits that will transform your life before 8 am*, Hal Elrod, *Hodder and Stoughton General Division*, 2017

Chapter 6

- *The Extreme Art of Self Care*, Cheryl Richardson, Hay House, 2009

- *Mama Gena's School of Womanly Arts*, Simon & Schuster, 2003

- *The Disease to Please: Curing the People Pleasing Syndrome*, Harriet Braikens, *McGraw-Hill Education*, March 2002

Chapter 7

- *The Young Professionals guide on how to prevent burnout*, Susan Scott, Filament Publishing, 2017

- *The European Food Safety Authority,* https://www.efsa.europa.eu/

- https://www.nutrition.org.uk

- Nicki Williams, *Happy Hormones for Life,* www.happyhormonesforlife.com

Chapter 8

- *The Expansion Game: A powerful method to transform your fear into brilliance,* Gosia Gorna, Conscious Dreams Publishing, September 2017, www.gosiagorna.com

- *Timinology, How to Manage your Thoughts, Live a Happy Life, Embrace Mindfulness and Learn to Love Yourself,* Tim Leach, March 2017

- *When I Loved Myself Enough,* Karen McMillen, Board book, 2001

Chapter 9

- *Jane Fonda & Lily Tomlin: A Hilarious celebration of lifelong female friendship*: Ted Women, December 2015, https://www.ted.com/talks/jane_fonda_and_lily_tomlin_a_hilarious_celebration_of_lifelong_female_friendship

- *Why Women need a Tribe,* Uplift Magazine, Tanja Taljaard & Azriel Re'Shell, March 2016, www.upliftconnect.com

- Motherly motherhood magazine, *Mama, you can't do it all so please delegate,* Liza Druxman, 2018, https://www.mother.ly/life/mama-you-cant-do-it-all-so-please-delegate

Recommended Additional Reading

- *The Expansion Game*, Gosia Gorna,
  Conscious Dreams publishing, 2017

- *The Miracle Morning: The six habits that will transform your life before 8 am*, Hal Elrod, John Murray Learning, 2017

- *Tired but Wired, How to overcome your sleep problems: the essential toolkit*, Dr Nerina Ramlakhan, Souvenir Press, 2013

- *Fast Asleep, Wide Awake: Discover the secrets of restorative sleep and vibrant energy*; Dr Nerina Ramlakhan, November 2016, Harper Collins Publishers

- *Happy Hormones for Life*,
  Nicki Williams, www.happyhormonesforlife.com

Softer Success Workshop Feedback

The tips and tricks in this book are just some of the strategies and tools that I teach in my workshops and 1-2-1 coaching sessions. Below, you will find participants feedback after working with me. I hope this will demonstrate clearly, that you can improve your situation by taking actions towards a Softer Success in your life too.

"What a brilliant workshop! In a time where mental health and burnouts are an epidemic this is really going to make a difference."
Caitlin Smith, Delivery Lead Equal Experts

"Thank you for the session today. Incredible to see how movement, visualisation, refocus to let go can help you! Cara's three ways to avoid burnout were simple and effective."
Laura Conrardy, Manager Customer Success, Box

"I think that lots of women would benefit from the techniques we learned about in Cara's workshop today."
Yolanda Mouriz, Personal Assistant, AKO Capital LLP

"I liked the exercises and feel they were simple enough for me to repeat them. I like to be with people at work as this will help us be mindful together."
Isabel Fernandez Alvarez,
Customer Success Portfolio Manager, Box

"In taking Cara's course I have learned techniques I can use in my busy job to help give release as well as help with insomnia caused by business."
Catrine Hostrup, Executive Recruiter Financial Services

"Very relaxing. Cara's session helped me focus on me and helped me take time out of the busyness of life."

Rebecca Hunt, Actor

"Excellent workshop. Cara made everything feel totally achievable. Put things in real actionable steps."

Chloe Williams,
Customer Marketing Specialist, Box EMEA

Acknowledgements

There are so many people I want to thank for their help with writing this book.

To my husband Joaquim, the love of my life. You have encouraged and advised me through this whole process. Thank you for being who you are.

To my darling little girls. I love you both to the moon and back.

My wonderful parents, Simon and Pella, for supporting me every step of the way.

To my sister Claire and cousins all around the world. Thanks for championing me.

My coach Gosia Gorna for without Gosia this would not have been possible. You have helped me transform my loose ideas into an amazing new career.

My book coach, Wendy Yorke who guided me to write this book with such patience and positivity. Thank you from the bottom of my heart.

Tim Leach – you gave me my first author tips – I love Timinology – thank you.

My tribe of Softer Success ladies. This book is for you!

My support group Maz, Cait, Edel, Aud; catching up with you guys is soul food.

Mama posse; I love how we support and cheer each other on.

SW1 group – thank you for being a great network and a huge help in the early days of motherhood.

Catrine, you are a connecting queen.

Caroline, who I first shared the chocolate raisin story with.

Elisabeth, for taking a first shot at reading this book.

Rosa, you are like a sister to me. Thank you for being who you are.

Zofia, for being there from the other side of the world.

Onvermeidelijk, we have seen each other through 25 years of fun and games. Thank you for laughing at my jokes or pretending to! Also, the 14 *Karaats* Ladies Hockey Team; we are all gold really.

Fran Borg Wheeler for editing.

Dr Nerina Ramlakhan for such an inspiring foreword.

Joe Cowens

To my wonderful case study ladies. Thank you for letting me share your stories.

Oksana Kosovan for all your hard work and patience during the typesetting stage.

Claire Lockey for press release and promotions.

Huge big thanks to Daniella Blechner from Conscious Dreams Publishing for staying on top of things and making for a smooth publishing process.

About The Author

Cara de Lange is an international wellbeing mentor, coach and speaker. *"I'm passionate about teaching people to become more gentle with themselves, change their mindset, avoid burnout."*

Her powerful techniques and tips, based on her studies, research and experimentation, are transforming the lives of hundreds of people. Her program **Prevent Burnout, Find Balance** enables individual clients and corporate teams to create a more harmonious, peaceful and productive life. In this book she shares some of these tried and tested techniques so that you too can slow down, increase your energy and become more resilient.

Cara brings a very international background to her work making it applicable to people around the world. Raised in the Netherlands and schooled in Belgium, Cara has also lived in South Africa, worked in Australia (for the Olympic Games in Sydney) and in New Zealand. She now lives with her Spanish husband and children in London.

Her corporate career, as a high powered Executive Assistant, spanned 20 years mainly in fast-paced, multi-national advertising and global technology companies such as Google (where she spent 11 years), Reckitt Benckiser, Saatchi & Saatchi. It was these corporate experiences that sowed the seeds for her current work. Seeing colleagues suffer overwhelm, high stress levels and burnout started her on the path to helping people heal. But it was her own full-blown burnout in 2015 that acted as the catalyst to leave behind her successful, international career and establish her own business, **Softer Success**, dedicated to helping people slow down, tune in and develop wellbeing strategies. *"My burnout was devastating but it was a wake call and paradoxically lead me to discover my life's work and passion. I truly hope my book will bring you the support and healing that you seek and deserve."*

Cara is an associate of and works closely with the International Stress Management Association (ISMA). She is also a member of the organising committee for International Stress Awareness Week. She speaks five languages: Dutch, English, French, German, and Spanish.